D1024751

PRESENTED TO:

_____

FROM:

_____

DATE:

_____

Product developed by Bordon Books, Tulsa, Oklahoma.
Manuscript written in association with Bordon Books by Rick and Melissa
Killian, Killian Creative, Boulder, Colorado.
Edited by Diane Stortz and Rayné Bordon.
Cover design by Koechel Peterson and Associates.

Published by Bethany House Publishers
11400 Hampshire Avenue South
Bloomington, Minnesota 55438

Bethany House Publishers is a division of
Baker Publishing Group, Grand Rapids, Michigan

Printed in the United States of America

ISBN-13: 978-0-7642-0288-9
ISBN-10: 0-7642-0288-X

13 12 11 10 09 08 07   9 8 7 6 5 4 3 2 1

The
Prayers
of
David

BECOMING A PERSON AFTER
GOD'S OWN HEART

BETHANYHOUSE
MINNEAPOLIS, MINNESOTA

Contents

Thou hast made us for Thyself, and the heart of man is restless until it finds its rest in Thee.

St. Augustine

Introduction

David began his story rather inauspiciously—by being overlooked.

Samuel, God's prophet in Israel, had arrived at the home of Jesse the Bethlehemite. God had told Samuel that Israel's next king would be found among Jesse's sons. But Samuel needed a cover, because King Saul was still alive and would want to kill Samuel if he found out that someone else had been anointed king. Samuel invited Bethehem's town leaders and Jesse and his sons to a feast in order to sacrifice to the Lord. David, however, wasn't even considered as a tagalong by his father or his brothers.

Instead, David remained out in the fields, where he kept watch over his father's sheep in the rolling hills near Bethlehem, unaware of the prophet's coming. He was sent for only when it was clear to Samuel that none of the rest of Jesse's sons were the Lord's choice to be king.

The hills where David cared for his sheep were the very same hills where, centuries later, other shepherds would watch by night and hear angels announce that Jesus, a very different kind of king, had just been born in Bethlehem—by that time known as the City of David.

While many of us may feel overlooked today, or unnoticed, we need to know that we can take heart from David's example. If he could rise from such obscurity to such prominence with God, so can we.

Wherever you are today, you need to know that you are neither alone nor forgotten. Others may have overlooked you, you may have had an unhappy childhood, you may have even reached your life goals yet feel lonelier than ever—but God is present and ready to respond to those who call upon Him—His help is always just a prayer away. Certainly you may not feel God's presence each time you call on Him, but you have His promise that He will answer. "This poor man cried out, and the LORD heard him, And saved him out of all his troubles" (Psalm 34:6 NKJV).

In view of this verse, studying the prayers of David can be beneficial when pressing into the full life God has promised. It is always helpful to learn from those who have traveled the road to knowing God before you, and David is among those who did it the best.

More than any other writings in the Bible, the prayers of David recorded in the book of Psalms reveal the intimacy, transparency, and friendship God desires with each of us. They portray the prayers of a man after God's own heart (1 Samuel 13:14)—revealing keys to knowing God that are as relevant today as when they were written generations ago.

The purpose of this book is not to break down these prayers of David in order to study their structure; it is to explore the nature of the God whom David knew. Even though we experience only David's side of the dialogue in his prayers, we also see the One David interacted with. Each chapter of this book looks at an aspect of God's character through David's eyes. The Lord was David's shepherd, his salvation, his passion, his refuge, his forgiver, his friend, and more. David's prayers teach us not so much how to pray and what to pray for but how to open up before God and experience Him in the fullness of His presence—a presence in which, according to David, the upright shall dwell (Psalm 140:13) and where there is protection from enemies (see Psalm 9:3; 17:2; and 31:20), great blessing (see Psalm 21:6), and "fullness of joy" (Psalm 16:11).

In addition to learning about God's character as we reflect

on these prayers, we also see David's character. At different times during his life, David was a lowly shepherd, a hero, a fugitive, an adulterer and murderer, and Israel's greatest king until Jesus came—yet he is remembered for none of these as much as for being a man who pursued God with his whole heart. David's prayers challenge us to become people who also pursue God's own heart diligently. If there is anything we can learn from David's life and his prayers, it is that no matter where we are now, no matter what our occupation or status in life is, we can also end up as people "after God's own heart," if we follow David's example. God invites us to pursue Him and to know Him in a direct invitation noted in Psalm 27:8, "You have said, 'Seek my face.'" David answered that invitation again and again, and it became his primary quest in life. In Psalm 63:1 he attests to that lifelong pursuit, "O God, you are my God; earnestly I seek you; my soul thirsts for you; my flesh faints for you, as in a dry and weary land where there is no water."

We see David coming to God in the morning, at noontime, and in the evening. Even during the middle of the night when others would be sleeping, he was pouring his heart out to God in painstaking honesty, in worshipful praise, and in deep reverence. It is those prayers of David's heart that challenge us to press in to know God more intimately ourselves. They teach us more than anything else about hungering for God and living in the presence of God.

Now it's your turn. As David answered the invitation to seek God as his best and trusted friend, the same invitation is issued to you, the reader. Are you ready to begin?

The LORD is my shepherd, I shall not be in want.
He makes me lie down in green pastures,
he leads me beside quiet waters,
he restores my soul.
He guides me in paths of righteousness
for his name's sake.
Even though I walk
through the valley of the shadow of death,
I will fear no evil,
for you are with me;
your rod and your staff,
they comfort me.
You prepare a table before me
in the presence of my enemies.
You anoint my head with oil;
my cup overflows.
Surely goodness and love will follow me
all the days of my life,
and I will dwell in the house of the LORD forever.

PSALM 23 NIV

I

THE LORD IS MY SHEPHERD

The day was quiet and bright as David puzzled over the melody and phrases of his latest song. He looked up and did a quick head count of the sheep as they munched lazily beside the stream. It was a habit he had acquired over the years. With little more than a glance to survey his flock and sense their mood, he knew immediately if any were missing or had strayed too far. He needed to be able to protect them if trouble bounded suddenly from the edges of the clearing. But everything seemed in order now.

For a moment longer, he let the gurgling of the running brook play upon his ear. A songbird warbled cheerfully in the distance; the sheep chewed and bleated softly to one another in the foreground. He would carry this picture of peacefulness with him all his life, though almost never would he experience it again: long hours that rolled into weeks of careful attentiveness over his father's flocks; days of sitting and pondering the nature of the universe and the God who created it, marveling at the intimate details of the grass beneath his feet and the utter magnitude of the sun and stars over his head.

> . . . HE SENSED THAT THE CREATOR OF ALL OF THIS—THOUGH GREATER THAN THE UNIVERSE ITSELF—WAS ALWAYS RIGHT THERE WITH HIM.

And somewhere in that stillness, with the edges of his heart, he sensed that the Creator of all of this—though greater than the universe itself—was always right there with him. A feeling so palpable that David wanted to reach out his hand and touch Him, but also so elusive that he knew simple, natural senses would never comprehend Him. But David was comforted to know that his Creator sat there with him, listening to the same stream, the same babbling of the sheep, and feeling the same light breeze that fingered the leaves of the myrtle trees and rippled the clear pool by which he sat. Yes, this was a moment of contentment.

David looked out over the sheep again. They seemed even more consumed by the stillness than he was; they didn't have a care in the world. From time to time, one looked up at him, wagging its head or baaing, as if to acknowledge David's protection—in the same way that David might view the shade of a tree on a hot day or the cover the tree provided in a sudden storm.

He set down his lyre for a moment and fingered the rod that hung at his belt, feeling its weight in his grip. Despite the peacefulness of the day, he knew that danger was never far away. Today wasn't all that different from the day a lion had stalked his sheep. If it had not been for his sling and the power of his rod, the lion might have done far more harm than simply spooking the sheep as it leaped from an embankment. David remembered catching that lion by the beard, bringing his rod down upon its head with a crack, and then pulling a badly frightened sheep from its mouth. God had certainly been with him! Had David's quickness been any less, it might not have been the lion that met his demise that day.

Then, of course, there was the bear that had been drawn by the sound of a bleating lamb that had fallen into a ravine. It took some well-placed stones to bring that great beast down. It also took some time for David to calm the lamb so that he could catch it in the crook of his staff, pull it from the pit, and return it to its mother.

With these memories strong in his mind, David turned his attention again to his lyre and began coaxing music once more from its strings.

David's most famous psalm starts with these simple lines:

> The Lord is my shepherd; I shall not want.
> He makes me lie down in green pastures.
> He leads me beside still waters.
> Psalm 23:1-2

Sheep are simple creatures, needing just four basic things to live: good pastureland, water, protection from predators, and guidance. David writes not only about having these necessities provided for him by his Lord and shepherd, but also about having the best of these. David understood that the Lord would lead him into lush "green pastures" and peaceful "still waters."

Yet human beings are more than sheep—we have souls—and in the next verse David reveals the effect of his shepherd's care on his spiritual nature.

He restores my soul.
He leads me in paths of righteousness
for his name's sake.
PSALM 23:3

Throughout all of the writings of David, there is a repeating principle: It is not in God's best interest to let those who follow Him go lacking or suffer at the hands of their enemies.

David knew that our character is our true wealth, and if you wanted to have an indication of the character of a man, you didn't look at the size of his house or the clothes that he wore—you looked to the state of his flocks, the health of his vineyards, and the contentment of his servants. A man might inherit a large home and be in debt for his fine clothes; it was his flocks, vineyards, and servants that showed the quality of his care and the diligence of his hand. If a landowner had sickly, raggedy sheep, what did that tell of this person's true character?

... IN DAVID'S ESTIMATION, ANY "GOD" WAS ONLY AS GREAT AS THE STATE OF HIS FLOCK OR THOSE WHO SERVED HIM.

So in David's estimation, any "god" was only as great as the state of his flock or those who served him. If the God of

Israel was the one true God—and David knew He was—then what kind of reputation would God have if everyone who followed Him were constantly sickly, needy, and destitute—especially spiritually? David saw that he had done nothing to deserve being led in God's paths of righteousness. Just the opposite! David's prosperity and quality of life were indications of God's faithfulness. If David was to lead his life as an example of how much better it is to live for God than to live for the world, wasn't it in God's best interest that he live an abundant life, not one marked by deprivation? The better David was cared for, physically and spiritually, the greater was his shepherd.

Jesus, the Good Shepherd

David somehow knew that just as he was watchful and attentive to his father's sheep, so God is watchful and attentive to us. In fact, David marveled continually at how often God thinks about us:

> You have multiplied, O Lord my God,
> your wondrous deeds and your thoughts toward us;
> none can compare with you!
> Psalm 40:5

How precious to me are your thoughts, O God!
How vast is the sum of them!
If I would count them, they are more than the sand.
I awake, and I am still with you.
Psalm 139:17-18

Believe it or not, God has been thinking about you just as He was thinking of David while he sat out in the fields watching the sheep, forgotten by the rest of his family. Are you directing your thoughts toward God just as David did, or are you distracted with something else?

John 9 tells the story of Jesus restoring the sight of a man who had been blind from birth. The religious leaders did not want to believe that Jesus had healed him on behalf of God. When they questioned the man repeatedly, he responded, "This is an amazing thing! You do not know where he comes from, and yet he opened my eyes. We know that God does not listen to sinners, but if anyone is a worshiper of God and does his will, God listens to him. Never since the world began has it been heard that anyone opened the eyes of a man born blind.

EVEN THOUGH THE BEGGAR WAS UNEDUCATED, HE RECOGNIZED JESUS AS A REPRESENTATIVE FROM GOD, UNLIKE THE RELIGIOUS LEADERS.

If this man were not from God, he could do nothing" (John 9:30-33). Even though the beggar was uneducated, he recognized Jesus as a representative from God, unlike the religious leaders. When Jesus told them that He had come to help the blind see, they wouldn't admit to their own blindness.

Speaking to these leaders, Jesus used words reminiscent of David's words in Psalm 23:

> Truly, truly, I say to you, he who does not enter the sheepfold by the door but climbs in by another way, that man is a thief and a robber. But he who enters by the door is the shepherd of the sheep. To him the gatekeeper opens. The sheep hear his voice, and he calls his own sheep by name and leads them out. When he has brought out all his own, he goes before them, and the sheep follow him, for they know his voice. A stranger they will not follow. . . .
> The thief comes only to steal and kill and destroy. I came that they may have life and have it abundantly. I am the good shepherd. . . . I know my own and my own know me, just as the Father knows me and I know the Father; and I lay down my life for the sheep.
> JOHN 10:1-5, 10-11, 14-15

Why does Jesus echo sentiments of David's prayer of praise? Because the Pharisees should have recognized who

He was through the works of care Jesus had done—just as a true shepherd would have done for his sheep. Jesus echoed this again in the gospel of Matthew: "Which one of you who has a sheep, if it falls into a pit on the Sabbath, will not take hold of it and lift it out? Of how much more value is a man than a sheep! So it is lawful to do good on the Sabbath" (Matthew 12:11-12). And in the gospel of Luke, Jesus says:

> What man of you, having a hundred sheep, if he has lost one of them, does not leave the ninety-nine in the open country, and go after the one that is lost, until he finds it? And when he has found it, he lays it on his shoulders, rejoicing. And when he comes home, he calls together his friends and his neighbors, saying to them, "Rejoice with me, for I have found my sheep that was lost." Just so, I tell you, there will be more joy in heaven over one sinner who repents than over ninety-nine righteous persons who need no repentance.
> LUKE 15:4-7

Jesus didn't use this language accidentally. He understood that if the Pharisees knew any of the psalms by heart, it would be David's shepherd psalm. He wanted them to realize what David knew: who God is can be seen in how He cares for His people. In Jesus' acts toward God's people, the Pharisees should have seen God's handiwork, but instead, they were blind to God's true goodness. Their pride, fear, and jealousy of Jesus kept them from seeing the truth about the One who wanted to be their shepherd.

The First Step toward Intimacy with God

God's goodness—His everlasting loving-kindness—runs throughout David's prayers. To realize that God cares for us and wants a genuine, intimate relationship with us is the first step toward knowing God as David did. Too many think of God only as a judge over their actions, forgetting or not understanding that through the cross we are forgiven and we can come to God's throne with confidence at all times (Hebrews 4:16).

> TO REALIZE THAT GOD CARES FOR US AND WANTS A GENUINE, INTIMATE RELATIONSHIP WITH US IS THE FIRST STEP TOWARD KNOWING GOD AS DAVID DID.

When we give our life to Jesus, God no longer sits in judgment over us. Jesus is now our advocate—defending us—and although God sometimes disciplines His children, He does not condemn or punish us. "There is therefore now no condemnation for those who are in Christ Jesus" (Roman 8:1). Instead, He blesses those who draw near to Him. As the author of Hebrews put it: "Whoever would draw near to God must

believe that he exists and that he rewards those who seek him"
(Hebrews 11:6).

Scripture tells us that God called Abraham His friend
(2 Chronicles 20:7) and the Bible says of Moses, "The LORD
used to speak to Moses face to face, as a man speaks to his
friend" (Exodus 33:11). But we don't know a great deal about
what Abraham and Moses said to God
during their conversations; we know
much more about what God had to say
to them. David's prayers in the psalms,
on the other hand, help us see what an
intimate friendship with God looks like
from our human point of view. To say
"The LORD is my shepherd," as David
says in Psalm 23, is to speak of a con-
stant walk with God under His loving and attentive care. God
leads us step by step; He knows where He wants to take us
next—and though there is often danger all around, His rod
and His staff are there to comfort us. Even if we face the "valley of the shadow of death," we have no need to fear, for God
has not led us there for our destruction but for the better pastures on the other side.

The benefits of following the shepherd as David expresses

> DAVID'S PRAYERS
> IN THE PSALMS
> HELP US SEE WHAT
> AN INTIMATE
> FRIENDSHIP WITH
> GOD LOOKS LIKE
> FROM OUR HUMAN
> POINT OF VIEW.

them in Psalm 23 are not something we wait to receive in the "sweet by and by" when we are in heaven. No, the benefits David writes of are for here in this life, for in heaven there will be no enemies opposing us, no dark valleys of death. David says that if we follow God's lead, His grace will always prove more than enough to see us through any trial or hardship. As the last two verses of this psalm express it:

> You prepare a table before me
> in the presence of my enemies;
> you anoint my head with oil;
> my cup overflows.
> Surely goodness and mercy shall follow me
> all the days of my life,
> and I shall dwell in the house of the LORD forever.
> PSALM 23:5-6

It is one thing to have a table set for us in the presence of friends and family, but how much more amazing to have a table set where our enemies can watch as God provides for us. Just as David knew there was constant danger around any watering place where he took his sheep, he also knew that there are enemies for anyone who lives as an intimate friend of God. Lions, wolves, and bears don't gather to hunt in barren places but near green pastures, because that is where the best prey will be found. When we place our trust in Jesus and allow God to be our shepherd, we discover that we also have enemies—both human and spiritual: "We do not wrestle against flesh and blood, but against the rulers, against the authorities, against the cosmic powers over this present darkness, against the spiritual forces of evil in the heavenly places" (Ephesians 6:12). But we need not fear—He will actually provide for us while we are in the midst of our enemies!

DWELLING IN THE HOUSE OF THE LORD— FOREVER

Abraham was called into the wilderness, Moses met God on the mountaintop, and Samuel heard the voice of the Lord in the tabernacle. David found God all around him by seeing with the eyes of his heart. Wherever we are, if we are willing to turn our attention to God, He will be found. We don't earn God's care and blessings by our behavior. We do need to give God our attention, our trust, and

> DAVID FOUND GOD ALL AROUND HIM BY SEEING WITH THE EYES OF HIS HEART.

our obedience in order to receive all He has for us, but His goodness and mercy are always following after us—pursuing us. The image is David's way of echoing the blessings of Deuteronomy: "All these blessings shall come upon you and overtake you, if you obey the voice of the LORD your God" (Deuteronomy 28:2).

God longs for a relationship with each of us that is marked by the same intimacy David expresses in Psalm 23. Whether we are in the midst of green pastures, beside still waters, or in the darkness of the valley of the shadow of death, He wants to walk with us every day—all we have to do is listen for His voice and follow our shepherd.

> *Know that the LORD, he is God!*
> *It is he who made us, and we are his;*
> *we are his people, and the sheep of his pasture.*
> PSALM 100:3

Father God,

What a great and good shepherd you are—completely able to take care of me! And I am so in need of you.

I'm frightened by what I hear on the news. I'm weary of days jammed with ceaseless activity; I'm hungry for what really matters, and I want to matter too.

But just like a sheep, I have a tendency to wander—trying to find my own way and my own solutions.

Help me to stop striving and lie down and rest. Point me in the right direction; I'll follow your lead. I won't worry about what I can't control; instead, I'll let you be in charge. When I'm afraid, remind me that you've promised to take care of me, and I'll watch to see what you're going to do.

Thank you for being my good shepherd. Help me to follow you with all my heart. Then may others see how good you are and want you to be their shepherd too.

Amen.

O LORD, our Lord,

how majestic is your name in all the earth!

You have set your glory above the heavens.

Out of the mouth of babes and infants,

you have established strength because of your foes,

to still the enemy and the avenger.

When I look at your heavens, the work of your fingers,

the moon and the stars, which you have set in place,

what is man that you are mindful of him,

and the son of man that you care for him?

Yet you have made him a little lower than the heavenly beings

and crowned him with glory and honor.

You have given him dominion over the works of your hands;

you have put all things under his feet,

all sheep and oxen,

and also the beasts of the field,

the birds of the heavens, and the fish of the sea,

whatever passes along the paths of the seas.

O LORD, our Lord,

how majestic is your name in all the earth!

PSALM 8

· II ·
The Lord Is My King

The king is disquieted. You have been asked to come and play your lyre for him," Jesse spoke without looking directly into David's eyes. He didn't really know what to make of his youngest son anymore. Not since the prophet Samuel had demanded that David join them and the rest of Jesse's sons to sacrifice to the Lord and to feast together—and then mysteriously anointed David with oil instead of one of his brothers.

What had it meant? Anointing was not done every day. Was David going to be a leader in Israel? But Saul was still king.

It had been a strange event. Though Samuel had made a great fuss about calling David, once David arrived and Samuel anointed him, Samuel said nothing more about it. He stayed a polite time with them afterwards, but his conversation was distracted. It was as if he badly wanted to be somewhere else. He seemed quite glad when he could finally make his exit. It was as if all he had ever intended to do was anoint David in a quiet ceremony and then get out of town before too many noticed he was there.

Jesse had always loved his youngest son, although the concerns of running his flocks and fields kept him from spending much time with David. He noticed that since Samuel's coming, David had changed. Favor seemed to follow him, and his brothers were growing jealous. Everything he set his hand to prospered. He was no longer a lad, unsure of himself. He was a young man. It was uncanny how David was growing up so fast, and how Jesse found it difficult to look him squarely in his piercing—and increasingly discerning—eyes.

And now this—King Saul asking for David to come and play his music to calm his nerves! Jesse knew it was a request he could not refuse, but he wondered where it would take his son next. He arranged for a donkey laden with bread, some smoked meat, and a skin of his best wine. He also tethered one of the finest goats to the donkey's saddle as a gift for the king.

David was both excited and unnerved to be called from his quiet days of watching sheep into the presence of King Saul. He knew little about Israel's royal court except that the king was to be obeyed without question and with the highest reverence. Saul had been chosen by God to lead Israel, and David believed it to be a great calling that deserved his deepest respect and devotion. He knew that as long as he lived, he must show this man nothing but honor and do him nothing but good.

> SAUL HAD BEEN CHOSEN BY GOD TO LEAD ISRAEL, AND DAVID BELIEVED IT TO BE A GREAT CALLING THAT DESERVED HIS DEEPEST RESPECT AND DEVOTION.

When he arrived at the palace, David was amazed at all the activity around it. There were tents nearby for the king's guards and soldiers; he heard the sounds of sheep, cattle, and goats in various pens. On the hills he could see pasturelands, new vineyards, orchards, and fields growing wheat and barley. All were cultivated with great care.

The palace itself was a simple building, two stories surrounded by a wall made from logs of cedar. David was met at the gate by soldiers, and then a servant took his gifts and led him to a tent to bathe and change into the fresh garments provided for him. Then David took up his lyre and was led to the throne room—which proved to be the entire lower floor of the palace.

The throne room's décor was as sumptuous as the palace's construction was simple. Intricate tapestries hung from the ceiling to divide the room into separate chambers. Foreign-looking pillows and furniture were arranged for sitting, and a magnificent throne stood imposingly centered along the broadest wall.

"This is David the Bethlehemite, your majesty," a page announced with some trepidation. All of the king's attendants seemed to want to keep from drawing his focus.

Then Saul looked at David. There was wildfire in Saul's eyes.

Beyond that intensity, though, David saw bitterness and anxiety. Rather than hold the king's gaze, David knelt.

"Play!" Saul choked out. "The rest of you,"—he waved his hand—"get out of my sight!"

David was led to a backless chair in the far corner of the room, where he quickly sat and positioned his lyre to do as he had been commanded. (See 1 Samuel 16.)

It is interesting to think that Israel's greatest king began his days in the palace court as an attendant—a simple bard. It appeared God was going to do things very differently with David than he had with Saul.

When the people of Israel called for a king to rule them so they could be like the other nations around them, God instructed Samuel to try to dissuade them, but he could not. So when God agreed to grant their request, He gave them a man they would have chosen for themselves—a man who, by his stature, was already head and shoulders above the crowd, and literally so; Saul was taller than all the rest—a man they could look up to.

Yet Saul was also proud and insecure. He respected his own will more than the directives of God. At Gilgal, when Saul saw his men growing restless and leaving because Samuel looked to be a no-show—he was already seven days late—rather than wait and allow the sacrifice to be performed according to God's law, Saul performed the sacrifice himself. (See 1 Samuel 13:8-15.) Later, when God told Saul to go down and utterly destroy the Amalekites and all that they owned, Saul decided to capture the Amalekite king

> GOD WAS GOING TO DO THINGS VERY DIFFERENTLY WITH DAVID THAN HE HAD WITH SAUL.

alive instead, and he kept the best of the enemy's sheep and oxen too, supposedly "to sacrifice to the Lord" (1 Samuel 15:21). Saul's nonchalant and blatant disobedience grieved God, and He soon sent Samuel out to anoint the next king. This time the king would be someone who had, like Saul, a pleasing appearance, but also had the more-important right attitude of the heart.

Saul's arrogance left him broken. Unable to accept and deal with the consequences of his disobedience, he became a morose and tormented man. Although he would reign until his death, he knew that God had rejected him as king. His relationships with those in his court now were based only on suspicion, and he trusted those in his service less and less. Although he looked for a way to escape his torment, he never sincerely repented before God.

> SAUL'S ARROGANCE LEFT HIM BROKEN. . . . HE BECAME A MOROSE AND TORMENTED MAN.

Oddly, though, the only place he did find comfort was through a humble musician, filled with the very presence of God that Saul had struggled against.

COMING INTO THE PRESENCE OF THE KING

When Saul was told by some in his court about a young

Bethlehemite who was "skillful in playing, a man of valor, a man of war, prudent in speech, and a man of good presence, and the LORD is with him" (1 Samuel 16:18), Saul hoped for little more than a respite from his violent mood swings. Instead, unknowingly, he brought God's next anointed king into the palace.

Had David been motivated by power, he might have viewed this as an opportunity to make a name for himself and to begin to build his future. We are never told how much he understood about his anointing by Samuel, or when he grasped its significance. Knowing David's humility, though, it seems unlikely that he would have sought to exalt himself even if he did know that he would someday be king. When David came into the palace, he came merely as a humble servant into the presence of royalty, with no ambitions beyond doing what he had been called there to do.

What an intimidating atmosphere the palace must have been for him, a simple shepherd from a small town. He must have come before Saul with the greatest respect and reverence, and probably not just a little apprehension. Despite his flaws, Saul was still king and his word was law. To disobey was treason; to obey was to gain favor and reward.

In the presence of Saul, David must have felt the fear any of us would experience when facing a king—the person who could have us killed by simply speaking a word. But David was not intimidated. He knew he was in covenant with the ultimate King—God himself! Although he showed great respect for Saul, his earthly king, he recognized that final authority and power rest with God.

The Beginning of Wisdom

David learned firsthand what it means to come into the presence of a king. He learned first that a king can be generous and full of blessing toward those upon whom his favor fell. David experienced this quickly as Saul took him into his immediate service as a musician and armor bearer even before he faced Goliath. In fact, had he not already won the respect of the king while in his service, it seems unlikely Saul would have let this young shepherd face the notorious giant with Israel's sovereignty on the line.

Yet, in Saul's throne room, David also learned that a king who didn't follow the Lord, could be tyrannical, self-possessed, and, at times, dangerous. Still, David knew Saul's power was insignificant compared with the power of the God who created the universe. He recognized that even a king had no power over him unless God granted it. Although he respected Saul greatly, he respected God more—this God who weighs oceans in the palm of His hand, levels mountains with the slightest gesture, and in whose breath is life itself. To be in the presence of such awesome power is never to be taken lightly. As the prophet Isaiah wrote:

> *Thus says the LORD:*
> *"Heaven is my throne,*
> *and the earth is my footstool;*
> *what is the house that you would build for me,*
> *and what is the place of my rest?*
> *All these things my hand has made,*
> *and so all these things came to be, declares the LORD.*
> *But this is the one to whom I will look:*
> *he who is humble and contrite in spirit*
> *and trembles at my word."*
> ISAIAH 66:1-2

The contrast that David would learn to see between Saul and the true Lord would only increase David's confidence in God. While the king of Israel was corrupt, selfish, and unpredictable in administering his authority, the King of heaven was just, full of loving-kindness, and always true to His Word. David became even more convinced that God can always be trusted to do what is right.

In addition, David gleaned valuable insight into what qualities make a great king. As he compared the way God rules with the way Saul ruled, the difference between justice and injustice was confirmed more firmly to him.

> BY GLORIFYING GOD THROUGH HIS PRAYERS AND PSALMS, DAVID EARNED FAVOR WITH BOTH HIS EARTHLY KING AND HIS HEAVENLY KING.

But even though David saw the hypocrisies in Saul's leadership style, he still entered King Saul's throne room much like he would enter the throne room of God—with a reverent heart of gratitude and a song of praise upon his lips. By glorifying God through his submissive attitude, David earned favor with both his earthly king and his heavenly King. He humbled himself before both and was soon promoted by both.

As we read in the book of Proverbs, "A man's gift makes room for him and brings him before the great" (18:16), and so David was brought before the king. He played his lyre to quiet the frenzies of an anguished heart—and as he did so, he not only serenaded King Saul but God himself.

I will sing a new song to You, O God;
On a harp of ten strings I will sing praises to You,
The One who gives salvation to kings.
PSALM 144:9-10 NKJV

THE HEART OF A TRUE KING

David's early experience as a shepherd faithfully looking after his father's sheep and then as a member of Saul's court, humbly ministering to the king, certainly prepared his heart to be the kind of leader God was calling him to be: a godly leader with a passion for service. In the words of Jesus, "If anyone would be first, he must be last of all and servant of all" (Mark 9:35). This was the path of training God had prepared for David toward one day being the king through whom He could bless His people. As Proverbs 15:33 NIV states, " … humility comes before honor." David had learned to humble himself before another king, all before he himself could be a king.

God saw in David a modesty and brokenness that made

WHAT PREPARED DAVID MOST FOR THE ROLE GOD WOULD HAVE HIM PLAY WAS HIS ABILITY TO SUBMIT AND SERVE WITH A FAITHFUL AND COURAGEOUS BOLDNESS, EVEN IN THE FACE OF AN UNRIGHTEOUS, UNREASONABLE SOVEREIGN.

him fit for His use. What prepared David most for the role God would have him play was his ability to submit and serve with a faithful and courageous boldness, even in the face of an unrighteous, unreasonable sovereign. David was willing to yield, while at the same time his fierceness and tenacity in service of the greater cause—the defense of Israel—went unmatched. It was within such character that God could reside—it was within such a heart that the King of the universe could make His home:

> *Thus says the One who is high and lifted up,*
> *who inhabits eternity, whose name is Holy:*
> *"I dwell in the high and holy place,*
> *and also with him who is of a contrite and lowly spirit,*
> *to revive the spirit of the lowly,*
> *and to revive the heart of the contrite."*
> Isaiah 57:15

David would put it this way:

> *O Lord, open my lips,*
> *and my mouth will declare your praise.*
> *You do not delight in sacrifice, or I would bring it;*
> *you do not take pleasure in burnt offerings.*
> *The sacrifices of God are a broken spirit;*
> *a broken and contrite heart,*
> *O God, you will not despise.*
> Psalm 51:15-17 niv

Not until Jesus himself came to dwell among us would there be such a fine example of a servant leader. David became Israel's finest king by serving the God he loved and loving the people he served with selfless abandon. He didn't see his role as king requiring the multitudes to serve him; his role was to lay down his life on behalf of those God had placed in his trust. Just like the Good Shepherd, he would do everything within his power to defend and protect all those entrusted to him, and to uphold the honor and glory of God for all to see. He had learned many valuable lessons while taking care of his father's sheep, which prepared him to be a good shepherd for God's people.

ONE KING OF ALL

The Lord was David's unquestionable king. David submitted himself continually to His higher authority. Although throughout his life he endured circumstances that challenged his hope and trust in God, he always remained steadfast. When David sinned, he went to God. When he was victorious, he went to God. All of his enemies were vanquished—every time David prayed and praised his God, his needs were met and the path before him cleared.

God ruled in the heart of this king. David hid himself in the shadow of the wings of the Most High (Psalm 63:7). David reached the place where God's will became his will, where he wanted nothing more than to please his King. Every Christian can experience this. When Jesus becomes our Lord, God places His kingdom within our hearts. As we follow Him, we experience peace, provision, protection, and prosperity—characteristics of His kingdom. David lived like that, and so can we.

King David's heroic feats were a result of his trust in an all-powerful God who also is, above all, good. David put his faith in the King of the universe. He gave glory where glory was due. He worshiped God continually, and God honored him. God proved to David that he could not trust too much, have hopes too high, or expect too much from his mighty King.

> The LORD sits enthroned over the flood;
> the LORD sits enthroned as king forever.
> May the LORD give strength to his people!
> May the LORD bless his people with peace!
> PSALM 29:10-11

Heavenly Father,

Your power is amazing. You spoke the universe into being. You sustain it by your word. Who am I to serve you?

Please help me learn what it means to bow to a king, because I'm so used to making my own decisions and going my own way. You deserve my allegiance.

Your Word tells me that you are good. As I follow you, may I see your goodness poured into my life. You are wisdom, and your ways are perfect. Help me to follow you today.

You are love. You paid the ultimate price to buy me back from the kingdom of darkness and bring me into your kingdom of light. Because of Jesus, I can come before your throne right now.

So here I am, God. Accept my praise and worship now, and lead me today.

Amen.

O LORD, how many are my foes!
How many rise up against me!
Many are saying of me,
"God will not deliver him."
    Selah
But you are a shield around me, O LORD;
you bestow glory on me and lift up my head.
To the LORD I cry aloud,
and he answers me from his holy hill.
    Selah
I lie down and sleep;
I wake again, because the Lord sustains me.
I will not fear the tens of thousands
drawn up against me on every side.
Arise, O LORD!
Deliver me, O my God!
Strike all my enemies on the jaw;
break the teeth of the wicked.
From the Lord comes deliverance.
May your blessing be on your people.
    Selah

PSALM 3 NIV

· III ·
The Lord Is My Salvation

David stooped next to the brook and let the cool water run through his fingers. He cupped his hands and took a drink, looking up at the horizon as the sun climbed toward midday. In this peaceful setting, it was hard to believe that a battle was brewing not far away. And in a short time, he would face Goliath, the greatest warrior of Israel's enemy—the Philistines.

Searching among the stones at the edge of the stream, he fingered those that had been tumbled and smoothed by the current. He knew the roundest would fly the straightest, and this was not the time to risk an errant shot. "Lord, you are my deliverer, my salvation in this time of need. Show me the right stones." No flaws. No rough spots.

Through the ripples in the stream, he saw a pebble that looked promising and bent down to pick it up. He spun it in his fingers to see if it was right. But it seemed a little lopsided, so he discarded it and picked up another.

His stomach tensed again as he thought of what was ahead. He wasn't without his doubts, but he also knew that God had never let him down. Even as David searched through the streambed, he felt God's presence as strongly as he ever had. Still, he couldn't help but wonder why no one else had stepped forward to accept the challenge of this Philistine, Goliath.

Certainly there was reason to be afraid—but how could there be any question that the Lord was greater than the false god of the Philistines? Was there any question that God would save Israel now, in this time of need, just as He had saved them in the face of the Egyptians at the Red Sea?

David smiled. The stone he had just picked up was perfect. He slipped it into his shepherd's bag. *Best to have others just in case*, he thought, and he continued his search.

He again remembered the lion and the bear. The initial sight of each had sent a blast of what felt like cold water through his veins, but he had not hesitated to act either time, knowing God was with him. It was only when the animal lay at his feet, dead, that he recognized the terrifying fear pulsing through his body. He knew there was no way he could have done what he did in his own strength and ability; God had guided his hand to salvation. He knew God would not abandon him this time either, especially considering that the flock he was defending now was the entire nation of Israel.

He found another suitable stone and slipped it into his pouch.

He looked up momentarily as he heard the rumble from over the hills of sword butts hitting shields. The armies had been lined up facing each other since morning, when he arrived to check on his brothers and bring them the supplies their father had sent.

And now here he was, preparing to take up the challenge of the Philistine's champion. David wondered at the arrogance of trusting in human strength alone. What was it like to live in a world like that? How could it end in anything but futility?

Another stone fit smoothly into the palm of his grip. He slipped it into his bag with the other two.

Could he bear a pagan world such as the Philistines lived

in, worshiping a false god and bullying other nations? In their world, strength and deception determined every outcome rather than righteousness and justice. He shuddered at the thought. *Don't they know the power of our God?* he wondered. *Don't they realize His justice will always prevail? Why would no one else in Israel stand up to this?*

He found two more rocks for his pouch side by side and decided five would be enough. He took a moment to kneel and pray again. "Lord, you are the God and protector of Israel, our salvation in time of need. Deliver this enemy into my hands today, that the earth will know there is a God in Israel. Make this giant an example so that all will know that the world will not be ruled with sword and spear but the battle belongs to you. Your righteousness cannot be overturned by the hands of men. Show the Philistines this day that even the least among your people can overcome any opposition as long as he trusts solely in you—you who are my ever-present salvation."

David rose and started walking toward the shouts and thundering of swords and shields on the other side of the hill.

It was time to face the giant. (See 1 Samuel 17.)

David would be not only Israel's finest king but also the nation's greatest hero—a hero of epic proportion. With God's help, Moses took on Pharaoh and parted the Red Sea, but David single-handedly killed a lion, a bear, and a Philistine giant. David was able to stand alone against his foes—alone with his God, that is—and overpower each one.

> DAVID WAS ABLE TO STAND ALONE AGAINST HIS FOES—ALONE WITH HIS GOD, THAT IS—AND OVERPOWER EACH ONE.

Undeniably, David had guts. With a stone and a slingshot, he brought down Goliath. Soon he would prove himself a fighting machine in hand-to-hand combat and lead a ragtag group of roustabouts against fearsome armies, emerging victorious against all odds time and again. He walked the earth as a man convinced of what his God could do for him.

THE GOD OF SALVATION

One has to wonder how David appeared to those he fought against and those he fought alongside. We know that he was "ruddy and had beautiful eyes and was handsome" (1 Samuel 16:12) and that he was "a man of good presence" (16:18). But how did David appear as he stood with five smooth stones in his shepherd's pouch, confidently facing his opponent as the only man in Israel who was willing to take on Goliath's challenge?

[DAVID'S] PRAISES WERE SHAMELESS IN THEIR EXUBERANCE BECAUSE HE KNEW THAT ONLY IN GOD COULD HE BE SO COURAGEOUS AND CONFIDENT.

Although we don't know more about what David looked like, we do know he put his trust in God. He was greatly favored and always successful because the Lord was with him. David knew where his salvation came from. He never hesitated to give glory and honor to God after every victory, after every fall, after every emotional low. His praises were shameless in their exuberance because he knew that only in God could he be so courageous and confident.

> I will extol you, O LORD, for you have drawn me up
> and have not let my foes rejoice over me.
> O LORD my God, I cried to you for help,
> and you have healed me. . . .
> Sing praises to the LORD, O you his saints,
> and give thanks to his holy name.
> PSALM 30:1-2,4

Without God, David was an ordinary man—but with God, David was one of the world's mightiest heroes.

PAINTING PORTRAITS OF SALVATION

When David described the salvation he saw in God, he used many different images. God's salvation is offered and experienced in a myriad of ways; for as many forms of trouble as there are, there is a salvation prepared by God to meet it. Whether victory in battle, physical healing, forgiveness for sin, or a need of the heart, God would save David by providing whatever was needed, and David knew this.

From the many facets of salvation David drew upon, he painted word pictures. In the stories he wove through his songs, David portrayed the salvation of God as a rock (2 Samuel 22:3), a tower (Psalm 61:3), a stronghold and a shield (2 Samuel 22:3), a horn (Psalm 18:2), and a cup (Psalm 116:13). Because he was able to put concrete images to his hope, he was able to convey that hope to others. David was a man of contagious hope.

DAVID WAS A MAN OF CONTAGIOUS HOPE.

We have heard it said that a picture is worth a thousand words. How quickly, when we hear "strong tower," are we able to understand the strength and protection of God? Perhaps David's word pictures of God's salvation helped him get his mind around all that God can be to us or helped him share what he understood about God's saving grace.

> *For who is God besides the LORD?*
>> *And who is the Rock except our God?*
> *It is God who arms me with strength*
>> *and makes my way perfect.*
> *He makes my feet like the feet of a deer;*
>> *he enables me to stand on the heights.*
> *He trains my hands for battle;*
>> *my arms can bend a bow of bronze.*
> *You give me your shield of victory;*
>> *you stoop down to make me great.*
> *You broaden the path beneath me,*
>> *so that my ankles do not turn.*
> *I pursued my enemies and crushed them;*
>> *I did not turn back till they were destroyed.*
> 2 SAMUEL 22:32-38 NIV

What greater trust could he put in the Lord? What more could David hope for—what more could he expect? He stirred his faith by putting into words all that he hoped from God. He framed his expectation and put feet to his hope through his continual praises, and God met him every time. God his strong tower—God his shield—God his rock—if such a God be for him, who could possibly prevail against him?

David, mighty man of valor, constantly reminded himself of this:

> The LORD is my rock and my fortress and my deliverer,
> my God, my rock, in whom I take refuge,
> my shield, and the horn of my salvation, my stronghold.
> PSALM 18:2

RAISING UP THE HORN OF SALVATION

As much as David was a warrior and a king, he was also a prophet. He spoke words about the God of salvation who one day would become flesh when Jesus, the Word, came to earth. "And the Word became flesh and dwelt among us, and we have seen his glory, glory as of the only Son from the Father, full of grace and truth" (John 1:14). The "horn of salvation" David sang of would one day be embodied in the King of Kings, the Lord of Lords, our hope of glory— Jesus Christ. Listen to the words of Zechariah from the gospel of Luke:

> Blessed be the Lord God of Israel,
> for he has visited and redeemed his people
> and has raised up a horn of salvation for us
> in the house of his servant David,
> as he spoke by the mouth of his holy prophets from of old,

> *that we should be saved from our enemies*
> *and from the hand of all who hate us;*
> *to show the mercy promised to our fathers*
> *and to remember his holy covenant,*
> *the oath that he swore to our father Abraham, to grant us*
> *that we, being delivered from the hand of our enemies,*
> *might serve him without fear,*
> *in holiness and righteousness before him all our days.*
> Luke 1:68-75

Jesus came to "give knowledge of salvation to his people ... because of the tender mercy of our God" (Luke 1:77-78) toward us. It is only because of God's mercy that we are able to experience all that God's salvation entails, all it encompasses. The salvation we are able to take hold of today is on account of God's great love for David and his offspring—Jesus—and all of us adopted into the household of God by grace through faith:

> *Great salvation he brings to his king,*
> *and shows steadfast love to his anointed,*
> *to David and his offspring forever.*
> 2 Samuel 22:51

It is difficult enough to comprehend the depth, height, length, and breadth of God's love. How much more impossible is it for us to fully understand the extent of God's salvation without the Holy Spirit enlightening us? The apostle Paul reminds us that "no eye has seen, nor ear heard, nor [has] the heart of man imagined, what God has prepared for those who love him" (1 Corinthians 2:9). Yet, Paul continues, the Spirit helps Christians understand salvation (v. 10). He helps us grasp the fact that it is not something for us to take hold of only in heaven, but something for us to also receive now as we allow ourselves to be transformed by the renewing of our minds by His truth (Romans 12:2).

> WE CAN MEDITATE ON ALL THAT GOD'S SALVATION ENTAILS . . . BUT IT IS ONLY BECAUSE OF GOD'S MERCY THAT WE ARE ABLE TO EXPERIENCE IT AT ALL.

The ram's horn represented power in its form as a sharp weapon; it also represented provision and healing as a cup that held wine or ointment, and it was an instrument used to lead troops into battle or to proclaim victory. David refers to God as his "horn of salvation" in both Psalm 18 and in 2 Samuel when speaking about God as his deliverer:

> My God, my rock, in whom I take refuge,
> my shield, and the horn of my salvation,
> my stronghold and my refuge,
> my savior; you save me from violence.
> 2 SAMUEL 22:3

Above all else, salvation refers to deliverance—deliverance from every conceivable trouble. David embraced that deliverance; he visualized it as a horn of salvation and all that represents—and so should we.

BECAUSE THEY TAKE REFUGE IN HIM

The salvation of God is available through the cross of Christ. Is that salvation conditional? What is our role in acquiring it?

All who would come to Christ must come in faith, taking refuge in Him alone. David declared that God delivers all who take refuge in Him. He tells us over and over that God will not deny His mercy to any who seek Him—that God's mercy and deliverance are available to all who trust and hope in Him.

> The salvation of the righteous is from the LORD;
> he is their stronghold in the time of trouble.
> The LORD helps them and delivers them;
> he delivers them from the wicked and saves them,
> because they take refuge in him.
> PSALM 37:39-40

We are made righteous in God's sight through our faith in Christ, and we are delivered and healed through that same faith. By trusting in God, we choose to declare His faithfulness as David did. All our expectations and all that we hope for are based on His promises, and we must confidently set our hope on Him. David was relentless in pulling on God's grace. He went to great lengths to prove his trust in God, and his tenacity pleased God. David went after God much like he did the lion, the bear, and the giant.

> Answer me, O LORD, for your steadfast love is good;
> according to your abundant mercy, turn to me.
> Hide not your face from your servant;
> for I am in distress; make haste to answer me.
> Draw near to my soul, redeem me;
> ransom me because of my enemies!
> PSALM 69:16-18

David spoke with authority when he declared what God could do. He was confident in his proclamations. He knew that when God said something He would surely keep His word—David expected God to follow through! This Scripture confirms the power and reliability of God's words. "So shall my word be that goes out from my mouth; it shall not return to me empty, but it shall accomplish that which I purpose, and shall succeed in the thing for which

I sent it" (Isaiah 55:11). Therefore, when David cried out to God to save him, he knew his salvation was assured!

> O Lord, do not forsake me;
> be not far from me, O my God.
> Come quickly to help me,
> O Lord my Savior.
> Psalm 38:21-22 niv

Father God,

How I thank you for saving me and setting me free!

You are my safe place—my strong tower. When trouble comes, help me run straight to you, taking refuge in you and trusting you to provide all that I need.

You are my rock—unchanging. Give me grace to grasp that you always do what you say you will do. Help me stand confidently on your wonderful promises to deliver me.

You offer me your salvation by offering me yourself. Thank you for all you are to me. Thank you for Jesus and the depth of His love for me.

May I live today in the freedom of your salvation. Help me understand your truth and be changed by it. Show me how to walk in your paths and be healed.

Thank you that at the end of my life here on earth, I can live with you in heaven forever!

Amen.

I say to the LORD, "You are my Lord;
I have no good apart from you." . . .
The LORD is my chosen portion and my cup;
you hold my lot.
The lines have fallen for me in pleasant places;
indeed, I have a beautiful inheritance.
I bless the LORD who gives me counsel;
in the night also my heart instructs me.
I have set the LORD always before me;
because he is at my right hand, I shall not be shaken.
Therefore my heart is glad, and my whole being rejoices;
my flesh also dwells secure.
For you will not abandon my soul to Sheol,
or let your holy one see corruption.
You make known to me the path of life;
in your presence there is fullness of joy;
at your right hand are pleasures forevermore.

PSALM 16:2, 5–11

· IV ·
THE LORD IS MY FRIEND

David still felt uncomfortable in Saul's court. He thought it would never quite become home for him, and that living in the tents of Israel's army would always feel more comfortable than residing in the palace.

But none of that mattered right now. He had received a message that Jonathan, the king's son, had something important he wanted to discuss with David, so David had gone to see him immediately.

Entering Jonathan's chamber, he saw that a fine meal had been set out. Jonathan smiled when he sensed the urgency and concern on David's face. "Greetings, my friend. Thank you for coming."

David noted the use of the word friend in Jonathan's welcome. While some used it lightly, Jonathan did not.

Jonathan had watched as David took up Goliath's challenge to the army of Israel. He had listened as David talked with Saul. David's devotion to the God of Israel resonated with Jonathan. Although older than David, Jonathan felt the deep bond of a brother with him, and it was something he wanted to honor and protect.

"David, I love you like a brother." Jonathan paused for a moment in thought. "I want to join the destiny of our two families in covenant."

David was stunned. "Jonathan, you know everything that I have—as little as it is—is already yours."

Again Jonathan smiled. He took off his coat and set it on David's shoulders. "David, my father gave me this coat as a symbol of my rank as prince of Israel. I want you to have it. I ask that you take it as a symbol of our friendship, so that all who see you wearing it will treat you with the dignity and respect worthy of the office it represents."

David understood the symbolism and ritual associated with Jonathan's actions. It was an act of creating a covenant between two friends—the sealing of an alliance between themselves and their descendants, an alliance that not even death could break. In response, David took off his own jacket from beneath the one draped over him and placed it on Jonathan's shoulders. "Jonathan, in the same way, please take my coat, knowing that with it I pledge my family to always be joined to yours. We will be your covering in time of need. As long as I have two coats, if you have none, then one will be yours. As long as I have a tent or house to call home, so will you. Should any of your descendents have a need, as long as it is within my power, I will meet that need. All that I have is yours."

Continuing the covenant ritual, Jonathan gave David his armor and his sword. "My defense is your defense," Jonathan said to David. "My sword will always be yours to command. Your enemy shall be my enemy, and your ally mine as well."

"I accept this from you and pledge the same to you for myself and my house," David responded.

Jonathan crossed to a rack of weapons set near one end of the room. After hesitating a moment, he pulled what he deemed his best bow from among the others. "David, you know I love archery and am skilled with the bow. Take this as a symbol that my skills and abilities are always at your disposal if you should need them."

David bowed his head as he accepted the bow. He

had no sword or armor or bow to give Jonathan in exchange. For a moment he wondered how to respond, and then he reached to his side and pulled from his belt his sling and his shepherd's pouch. "I used these to defeat Goliath. They are reminders of the strength God gave me for that task. I want you to have them. They are a symbol of what I can do with God's help. Whatever your need may be, I offer my faith and skills to meet your need to the best of my ability."

The two men clasped shoulders in a bear hug. "David, break bread with me!" Jonathan said.

This time, it was David who smiled. "Of course, my friend! And the next time you are on the battlefield, you will eat in my tent. But as for now, I have to admit, I could use a meal after my travels!"

Both men laughed and sat down to enjoy the feast that Jonathan had commanded be set out for them.

In both the Old and New Testaments, friendship is used to illustrate a connection or relationship held together by a bond of intentional love—love not based on emotion but a commitment to continual, unbreakable devotion and goodwill toward the other. According to Proverbs 18:24, "There is a friend who sticks closer than a brother," words possibly recorded by Solomon as he remembered his father's stories about Jonathan.

NO GREATER LOVE

In the gospel of John we read, "Greater love has no one than this, that he lay down his life for his friends" (John 15:13 NIV), and in Proverbs we are told, "A friend loves at all times" (17:17). Jesus' command is that we should walk in this loving-kindness as He did:

> "My command is this: Love each other as I have loved you.
> . . . You are my friends if you do what I command. I no
> longer call you servants, because a servant does not know his
> master's business. Instead, I have called you friends, for every-
> thing that I learned from my Father I have made known to
> you. You did not choose me, but I chose you and appointed
> you to go and bear fruit—fruit that will last. Then the
> Father will give you whatever you ask in my name. This is
> my command: Love each other."
> JOHN 15:12, 14-17 NIV

In this passage, Jesus tells us that as our friend, He is willing to show His love for us by laying down His life for our sake. He then goes on to say that if we are His friend, then we will love others the same way.

As our friend, Jesus actually confides in us. He instills His purpose for each of us into our hearts and shares everything He has with us in support of accomplishing His will. A master would normally give his servants instructions that they are to follow without question and usually without knowing the ultimate goal of their actions. But Jesus wants us to be friends—co-laborers if you will.

GOD, IN EFFECT, IS LOOKING FOR PARTNERS TO SPREAD HIS TRUTH TO THE WORLD.

God, in effect, is looking for partners to spread His truth to the world. Partners—or friends—share the vision and purpose as well as the tasks, and the more God knows that we have hearts that love Him and long to obey Him, the more He will share with us as His friends. David expressed it this way:

> Who is the man who fears the LORD?
> Him will he instruct in the way that he should choose. . . .
> The friendship [secret counsel] of the LORD is for those who fear him,
> and he makes known to them his covenant.
> PSALM 25:12, 14

In the verses from John 15 quoted previously, Jesus says that He has told us everything the Father told Him. Jesus laid His heart bare and withheld nothing. He goes on to say that He chose us that we might represent Him—and as we do, whatever we will ask in His name the Father will do for us. The passage ends with a commandment, that we love one another selflessly, with the good of the other always in mind, as He loved us.

> MORE THAN ANY OTHER HERO OF FAITH, WE ARE TOLD ABOUT DAVID'S EPIC FRIENDSHIPS AND WHAT THOSE RELATIONSHIPS MEANT TO HIM.

That is how David loved those who trusted him and whom he knew he could trust. David understood the value of friendship. He formed a long list of friends—including Abiathar, Nahash, Hiram, Hushai, Ittai, and Jonathan—to whom he showed extraordinary kindness and loyalty. More than any other hero of faith, we are told about David's epic friendships and what those relationships meant to him. He never underestimated the value of a faithful companion.

A FRIEND OF GOD

David made God his closest confidant and most trusted

ally, even as God considered David a man after His own heart. David knew the potential inherent in a covenant relationship, and he trusted God more than anyone else. In return for pledging his allegiance to God—for loving Him with all of his heart, soul, mind, and strength—David knew he could depend on God. Because he knew that God was indeed mindful of him, that He knew him inside and out, David counted on God's fidelity in everything he did. Yes, God was his loving Father who had knit him together in his mother's womb, but He also was a faithful friend with whom David could share his troubles and count on for help and wisdom in times of trouble. David could lean on the Lord when he felt insecure, he could confide in Him when he knew he had sinned, and he could count on His company when he didn't have another soul in the world to stand with him.

DAVID EXERCISED HIS ADMIRATION FOR GOD'S LAWS IN HIS DEVOTION TO PRAISING AND WORSHIPING GOD AT ALL TIMES.

Neither did David take for granted being God's friend. He knew intimacy with God is reserved for those who fear the Lord. Therefore David clung to the law of his Lord and sought to obey Him in every situation. David exercised his admiration for God's laws in his devotion to praising and worshiping God at all times. He always opened his heart in prayer, asking God to show him any waywardness in himself so that he could correct it.

> *Search me, O God, and know my heart;*
> *test me and know my anxious thoughts.*
> *See if there is any offensive way in me,*
> *and lead me in the way everlasting.*
> PSALM 139:23-24 NIV

> *Declare me innocent from hidden faults.*
> *Keep back your servant also from presumptuous sins;*
> *let them not have dominion over me!*
> *Then I shall be blameless,*
> *and innocent of great transgression.*
> *Let the words of my mouth and the meditation of my heart*
> *be acceptable in your sight,*
> *O LORD, my rock and my redeemer.*
> PSALM 19:12-14

God coaches and counsels those who love and trust Him as David did. David was a devoted student of God's law and sought to please the Lord by being quick to heed it at all times— as well as apologize and ask forgiveness when he violated it. David couldn't bear the thought of breaking God's confidence in him. The more time he spent with God, the more he longed to fully know His ways and see His face.

David's idea of friendship was much more than the casual relationship we use the term to describe today, much more than a mere acquaintance. It was marked by a commitment greater than being a brother and called for a commitment to kindness and looking out for the interest of the other beyond even that of a legal partnership. David found a balance between relating to God with the reverence and fear due His kingship and the commitment and intimacy of being His friend. If we are to be people after God's own heart, as David was, it is a balance we need to find in our personal relationship with God as well.

> *Let us then with confidence*
> *draw near to the throne of grace, that we may receive mercy*
> *and find grace to help in time of need.*
> Hebrews 4:16

Heavenly Father,

I offer you my praise and worship today because of who you are and all that you have done for me. Thank you for being my friend.

You sent your Son, Jesus, to lay down his life for me. There's no greater demonstration of love that anyone could make than your willingness to save me like that.

You are my perfect friend, Father. You have promised never to leave me on my own. You guide and direct me, and you care about every detail of my life. And like a true friend, you show me where I need to change and grow. Look at my life today, Lord, and point out my faults and tell me how to address them. Let me see where my heart is not wholly focused on you.

As my friend, you even confide in me—how amazing! You have shared with me your desire that everyone might be saved by trusting in Jesus Christ. You have called me to be part of your plan of salvation by reaching out to others with your good news. Help me see where I fit in that plan today and what you want me to do.

May I be a friend to others today, Lord, like you are a friend to me, so they can know that you want to be their friend too.

Amen.

For God alone my soul waits in silence;
from him comes my salvation.
He only is my rock and my salvation,
my fortress; I shall not be greatly shaken. . . .
For God alone, O my soul, wait in silence,
for my hope is from him.
He only is my rock and my salvation,
my fortress; I shall not be shaken.
On God rests my salvation and my glory;
my mighty rock, my refuge is God.
Trust in him at all times, O people;
pour out your heart before him;
God is a refuge for us.
    Selah

PSALM 62:1–2, 5–8

The LORD is my light and my salvation;
Whom shall I fear?
The LORD is the defense of my life;
Whom shall I dread? . . .
Though a host encamp against me,
My heart will not fear;
Though war arise against me,
In spite of this I shall be confident.

PSALM 27:1, 3 NASB

· V ·

✝ THE LORD IS MY CONFIDENCE

David examined the rolling hills not far from Saul's palace for what he felt would be the last time. His face was still wet and he wiped his eyes again in vain. Without thinking, he scanned the rocky outcroppings of the hills for possible ambushes and then began working his way up to the crest of the hill before him. He hoped he could follow this for a good distance while keeping out of sight. At times he glanced nervously behind him, fearing he was being followed. His heart felt like it hung broken within him; the ache made it hard to breathe.

Despite Jonathan's attempts to comfort him, David was

crestfallen. To the best of his ability—as a soldier, a musician in his household, and even as a son-in-law—David had served Saul with all of his heart and strove to make his house great. Saul's throne had never been more secure, and David had never shown him anything but the deepest loyalty. Saul, however, remained envious and bitter—and that bitterness only grew each time David accomplished another great feat in Saul's cause. And now, after meeting Jonathan out in these fields where he had been hiding, David knew for certain that his father-in-law wanted him dead.

Until today, David had believed he would always dwell in the house of Saul. With Saul's son Jonathan being closer than his own brothers, and Saul's daughter Michal his wife, David was finally beginning to feel like he belonged in the royal court. He had indeed looked to Saul as a father and leader, yet the more he did to serve him, the shorter Saul's patience grew with David as envy and paranoia ate away at him.

David knew his only chance now was to flee into the mountains and villages that had been his home during his many campaigns to protect Israel from attacking nations. As he had learned from his soldiering, he would have to survive with only what he could carry, leaving everything else behind. He thought momentarily of Michal—he hadn't even been

THE LORD IS MY CONFIDENCE ✦ 75

able to say good-bye. He knew she would be safe in her father's house and that his new life of exile would not be one she could embrace. He wondered if he would ever see her again.

Then he realized that it wasn't just his wife he had lost, but everything. He would never be able to return to his home again, and all that he had earned, all that he had stored away for the future, everything he had won in battle, everything he had hoped for—it all was gone. He couldn't even return to his father's house in Bethlehem for fear that it might bring Saul's anger down on Jesse and his sons.

Topping the ridge, David stopped. *Where will I go?* He wondered about returning to Samuel to hide again in Ramah, but that would be no better than returning to Bethlehem. For a moment he took in the surrounding landscape and weighed his options. *Where can I go?* He thought again. *Who can I trust?*

Trust. A tough word at the moment. All that David had trusted was now gone—his home, career, family, wealth—everything.

Not everything.

David wondered a moment at this stray thought.

Not the Lord.

A prayer formed in David's mind:

> The LORD is a stronghold for the oppressed,
> a stronghold in times of trouble.
> And those who know your name put their trust in you,
> for you, O LORD, have not forsaken those who seek you.
> Sing praises to the LORD, who sits enthroned in Zion!
> Tell among the peoples his deeds!
> For he who avenges blood is mindful of them;
> he does not forget the cry of the afflicted.
> PSALM 9:9-12

Yes, he thought, *the Lord is still with me!*

> When I am afraid,
> I put my trust in you.
> In God, whose word I praise,
> in God I trust; I shall not be afraid.
> What can flesh do to me?
> PSALM 56:3-4

His tears finally stopped. His heart rose again. *I am the Lord's. Why am I worrying? I am His—I wonder what He is going to do with me now?*

For the first time in days, a smile crept across his face.

He checked his gear, took a sip of water, thought about a spring he knew was not far away where he could refill his water skin, and set off with new confidence. A song rose from within him, and he began to sing aloud.

He was ready for whatever his journey might bring him next.

David knew he belonged to God, and as long as he put his faith in God, God's perfect will would be done in his life. God was his strength, his wisdom, his protection, and his deliverance. He knew that it was God who defeated the lion and the bear. He recognized that it was the presence of God that came when he played his lyre to calm Saul's fits and God who gave him favor in the king's sight. It was God who had defeated Goliath and it was God who had protected him and defeated the tens of thousands of enemies that won him the honor and notoriety behind Saul's jealousy. David knew that it was all God before, not him, so now that it all had been taken away, what was really different? Why should he be sorrowful?

DAVID'S FOUNDATION FOR CONFIDENCE

David could look at the amazing turns of his life and say that he never deserved any of them; all the honor belonged to God anyway, so if God was going to let it all be taken away from him, why should he fret? David knew that God was in control and would take care of him:

> The steps of a good man are ordered by the LORD,
> And He delights in his way.
> Though he fall, he shall not be utterly cast down;
> For the LORD upholds him with His hand.
> PSALM 37:23-24 NKJV

This confidence also came from David's knowledge of God's law and His promises. He knew that the righteous could not be kept down for long and that God would never allow evil to have the last word. He hid God's words in his heart, and he knew "the testimony of the LORD is sure" (Psalm 19:7). There are other places in the Bible to read about the benefits of following God's law, but none of them celebrate God's commandments quite as David did:

> The words of the LORD are pure words
> like silver refined in a furnace on the ground,
> purified seven times.
> You, O LORD, will keep them;
> you will guard us from this generation forever.
> PSALM 12:6-7

> The law of the LORD is perfect,
> reviving the soul;

the testimony of the LORD is sure,
making wise the simple;
the precepts of the LORD are right,
rejoicing the heart;
the commandment of the LORD is pure,
enlightening the eyes;
the fear of the LORD is clean,
enduring forever;
the rules of the LORD are true,
and righteous altogether.
More to be desired are they than gold,
even much fine gold;
sweeter also than honey
and drippings of the honeycomb.
Moreover, by them is your servant warned;
in keeping them there is great reward.
PSALM 19:7-11

David knew that God's timing can be different than we would like it to be but that His promises are sure nonetheless. If God said He would do it, David would be the first to take that promise to the bank!

Knowing God Has a Purpose for Your Life

The Bible doesn't tell us when David understood clearly why Samuel had anointed him, but he had to have known it wasn't so he would die in obscurity at the hands of Saul. David risked great things because his heart told him there were great things to be accomplished. He knew that blessing was dependent on following God and that the best was still ahead for Israel if they would simply trust in His ways and follow His statutes.

> *I believe that I shall look upon the goodness of the* Lord *in*
> *the land of the living!*
> *Wait for the* Lord;
> *be strong, and let your heart take courage;*
> *wait for the* Lord!
> Psalm 27:13-14

When you know God has a purpose for your life and that you are walking in it—and you know God is doing everything He can to see you fulfill it—what is there that can overcome you? There is something about the audacity of trusting God beyond any circumstance that comes against you. Certainly there are times when we find ourselves at the wrong end of events and realize the need to get back on God's path if we ever hope to get out. But there also are times when circumstances derail us in the midst of our best seasons with God, and we mistakenly take it as a cue to give up.

David must have wanted to quit when he realized he could never again return to Saul—but he didn't. He must have been greatly tempted to turn his back on all he valued—fighting valiantly for Israel, honoring God's anointed king, and loving the Lord passionately—but David didn't give in. Instead, he stayed constant. He continued to fight for Israel wherever he could even though he was in exile. He refused to turn against Saul even when he had opportunity to do so, and he clung all the tighter to God's promises despite the fact that his faithfulness seemed to result only in frustration.

> THERE IS SOMETHING ABOUT THE AUDACITY OF TRUSTING GOD BEYOND ANY CIRCUMSTANCE THAT COMES AGAINST YOU.

While others despair in the face of calamities, David said:

> *Though I walk in the midst of trouble, . . .*
> *[t]he LORD will fulfill his purpose for me;*
> *your steadfast love, O LORD, endures forever.*
> *Do not forsake the work of your hands.*
> PSALM 138:7-8

No matter what happened, David simply said, "In You, O LORD, I put my trust; Let me never be ashamed" (Psalm 31:1 NKJV). There is something about trusting God even when there are no reasonable grounds to do so. This was definitely an attribute that exemplified David's life. Perhaps we could use more of it in our lives as well.

> *Though an army encamp against me,*
> *my heart shall not fear;*
> *though war arise against me,*
> *yet I will be confident.*
> Psalm 27:3

Father God,

It's so easy to trust you when my life is going well. I confess that when my circumstances are difficult, I have a hard time believing you are still taking care of me.

But when I look at the past, I can see that you have indeed been faithful to me. I have come through the hard times, and you are healing my wounds with your love.

So please help me, God! Increase my confidence! Help me choose today to believe what you say. You are always good, and you will never leave me alone. Help me to seek you in your Word. Remind me of your promises whenever I am afraid.

Your purpose for my life will not be overcome by evil if I remain committed to you. Help me when I waver, God!

Right now I give over to you every stressful situation that I face today. May my every action and response today show my confidence in you. Thank you for being my confidence. May others see today through me how faithful and good you are.

Amen.

Be merciful to me, O God, be merciful to me,
for in you my soul takes refuge;
in the shadow of your wings I will take refuge,
till the storms of destruction pass by.
I cry out to God Most High,
to God who fulfills his purpose for me.
He will send from heaven and save me;
he will put to shame him who tramples on me.
    Selah

Psalm 57:1–3

In you, O Lord, do I take refuge;
let me never be put to shame;
in your righteousness deliver me!
Incline your ear to me;
rescue me speedily!
Be a rock of refuge for me,
a strong fortress to save me!
For you are my rock and my fortress;
and for your name's sake you lead me and guide me;
you take me out of the net they have hidden for me,
for you are my refuge.
Into your hand I commit my spirit;
you have redeemed me, O Lord, faithful God.

Psalm 31:1–5

· VI ·
THE LORD IS MY REFUGE

D avid could hardly breathe.

He pressed himself flat against the wall of the cave, listening to the noises and voices just outside. How many men were out there? David and his men were well hidden, but how long would it be before they could leave?

Someone shouted orders and then ducked into the cave. David knew that voice—it belonged to Saul!

David nodded in the half-light for his men to withdraw deeper into the cave with him, where they could talk more freely. Even in the silence, he could tell that some of the others had also recognized Saul and knew that the one they were fleeing was now only a few feet away.

When they felt they were at a safe distance, it was David who spoke first. "He is only relieving himself. I don't think he will come in any further. We are safe for the time being."

His men nodded agreement. But several of them said, "David, this is our opportunity. Here is the day of which God said to you, 'Behold, I will give your enemy into your hand, and you shall do to him as seems good to you.'"

David considered these words for a moment, grateful the others could not make out his expression in the darkness. "Leave it in my hands. I am the outlaw here, not you. This is my fight." He rose, and staying in the shadow of a crevice at the base of one of the walls of the cave, he carefully made his way back to where Saul was.

He felt the eyes of his men behind him burrowing into his back from where they hid in the shadows, watching his every move.

From his hiding place, David could hear Saul's breath, smooth and even, as he sat motionless before him. Then he took his knife silently from its sheath, reached out, and sliced off a corner of Saul's robe.

After this, David made his way back to the shadows. He could literally feel the air leave as his men breathed out their astonishment—he had left Saul alive. Reaching the shadows again, he walked past his men into the depths of the cave.

David chose to speak before anyone else could question him. "God forbid that I should do this thing to our king. He is the Lord's anointed. I cannot put out my hand against him." His men murmured in response, and some among them offered to do the job for him. David's voice, though still a whisper, was stern in response. "What are we to expect of the Lord if we take it upon ourselves to destroy what He has established? Is God not great enough to handle His own problems? What protection is there for men who fight against God?"

The others quieted. They knew there was no answer to this. They made their way further into the cave and awaited Saul's departure.

When Saul left the cave and at last his army rose and departed, David and his men waited until they were a safe distance away before they climbed out from the cave. Then standing at the top of a cliff, David shouted after Saul and his troops: "My lord the king!"

When he saw Saul turn in his saddle, David bowed his head to the ground and called out, "Why do you listen to the words of men who say, 'Behold, David seeks your harm'? Look!" he cried, holding out the corner of Saul's robe.

Saul grabbed his robe, searching, until he found where a

piece was missing. He looked again toward David.

"This day your eyes have seen how God gave you into my hand in this cave. Some told me to kill you, but I did not harm you. I told them, 'I will not put out my hand against my king, for he is the LORD'S anointed.' See, my father, see the corner of your robe in my hand? For by the fact that I cut off the corner of your robe and did not kill you, you may see and know there is no wrong or treason in my hands. I have not sinned against you, though you hunt my life. Let God judge between me and you. Vengeance is the Lord's. As the proverb of the ancients says, 'Out of the wicked comes wickedness,' but my hand shall not be against you. After whom has the king of Israel come out? After a dead dog! After a flea! I am nothing that you should worry about. May God therefore be judge and give sentence between me and you, plead my cause, and deliver me from your hand." (See 1 Samuel 24:1-15, paraphrased.)

Very few of David's psalms are actually identified as being tied to specific events in his life. However, Psalm 57 (found at the beginning of this chapter) was written in response to his experience in the cave with Saul. "In the shadow of your wings I will take refuge, till the storms of destruction pass by" (Psalm 57:1).

Saul and his army were chasing David with the sole purpose of ending his life. Why didn't Saul have his men search that cave? Why didn't he hear David and his men moving around there? It had to be because David and his men were wrapped in God's protection—they were hidden in Him, kept invisible from those who would do them harm—safe and unreachable.

IN THE SHADOW OF HIS WINGS

David's continual prayers for protection and his trust in God to answer those prayers did not go unrewarded. We can hear David's gratitude for God's faithfulness to him in his words at the end of Psalm 57:

> My heart is steadfast, O God,
> my heart is steadfast!
> I will sing and make melody! . . .
> I will give thanks to you, O Lord, among the peoples;
> I will sing praises to you among the nations.
> For your steadfast love is great to the heavens,
> your faithfulness to the clouds.
> PSALM 57:7, 9-10

David spent years on the run from Saul, but he continually chose faith in God rather than fear. He chose to rise every morning and pray instead of fretting. He got up, took up his lyre, and then sang praises to his Lord and protector—day after day, week after week, and year after year.

> *Hear my cry, O God;*
> *Attend to my prayer.*
> *From the end of the earth I will cry to You,*
> *When my heart is overwhelmed;*
> *Lead me to the rock that is higher than I.*
> *For You have been a shelter for me,*
> *A strong tower from the enemy.*
> *I will abide in Your tabernacle forever;*
> *I will trust in the shelter of Your wings.*
> *Selah*
> Psalm 61:1-4 NKJV

God's protection doesn't necessarily mean that we won't meet danger, but even in the midst of the danger He will keep us safe. As a shepherd, David wrote in Psalm 23 about walking "through the valley of the shadow of death" and a table prepared "in the presence of [his] enemies." In Psalm 57, as a fugitive, he declared:

> *My soul is in the midst of lions;*
> *I lie down amid fiery beasts—*

the children of man, whose teeth are spears and arrows,
whose tongues are sharp swords.
Be exalted. O God, above the heavens!
Let your glory be over all the earth!
They set a net for my steps;
my soul was bowed down.
They dug a pit in my way,
but they have fallen into it themselves.
    Selah
PSALM 57:4-6

In the midst of danger, like Daniel in the lions' den, David was safe in God's arms—or as the psalm says, in the "shadow of His wings." In the face of peril, David's heart was steadfast. He knew that God was his place of safety, his fortress. He had seen God protect him many times before. Therefore, he chose to trust in God's protection rather than trying to kill Saul himself, even though that option may have looked like immediate deliverance.

> IN THE FACE OF PERIL, DAVID'S HEART WAS STEADFAST.

David's temptation in the cave—and on various occasions later—was to end Saul's threat by relying on his own strength. The suggestion to do so even came from his friends and sounded godly: "Here is the day of which the LORD said to you,

'Behold, I will give your enemy into your hand, and you shall do to him as it shall seem good to you'" (1 Samuel 24:4). Yet the act of raising his hand against God's anointed was anything but right in the sight of God. In this situation, as in so many others, David refused to rely on what human wisdom dictated when it proposed coming against anything God had established.

Does this suggest that we should not use all of our God-given abilities when we face a crisis? No. Many times when David faced his enemies, he defended himself without hesitation, fighting with every human skill he had to protect his nation. But he would not lift his hand in situations where delivering himself meant violating God's law. Instead he chose to trust in God as his refuge and place of safety.

DAVID CLUNG TO THE LORD, TRULY BELIEVING IN HIS HEART THAT GOD WAS HIS "PORT IN THE STORM" AND WOULD SAFELY BRING HIM HOME.

It may have looked as though David had been deserted and would sooner or later be destroyed by Saul and his men. But David clung to the Lord, truly believing in his heart that God was his "port in the storm" and would safely bring him home.

Amidst all the confusion and violence in our world today,

we too desperately need a place of refuge—a place of safety where we can hide until the storm passes by. It requires from us a willingness to trust in God's goodness as well as His ability to shelter us.

Most of us have little trouble in believing that God has the power to protect us. It's more a question of whether or not we believe He is willing. We sometimes have a suspicion of Him and His motives toward us. *Does He really want my good? Does He really care? Maybe He wants to punish me.*

Such attitudes reveal that we are viewing God through human eyes. Sometimes we are not trustworthy, so we think He must not be either. Or we think, *If we don't have good motives, maybe He doesn't.* But God is not like us—He is pure love—no evil intent whatsoever! And we can trust Him—all the time. He is always faithful and unswervingly trustworthy. Numbers 23:19 NIV confirms this: "God is not a man, that he should lie, nor a son of man, that he should change his mind. Does he speak and then not act? Does he promise and not fulfill?"

Are you experiencing storms in your own life right

> BUT GOD IS NOT LIKE US—HE IS PURE LOVE—NO EVIL INTENT WHATSOEVER! AND WE CAN TRUST HIM—ALL THE TIME.

now? The Lord wants to encourage you that He will be your refuge if you will let him. This is His promise to you:

> He who dwells in the shelter of the Most High
> will abide in the shadow of the Almighty.
> I will say to the LORD, "My refuge and my fortress,
> my God, in whom I trust." . . .
>
> A thousand may fall at your side,
> ten thousand at your right hand,
> but it will not come near you.
> You will only look with your eyes
> and see the recompense of the wicked
> PSALM 91:1-2, 7-8

Heavenly Father,

You wanted your children to live with you in a perfect world, and someday, in heaven, we will. But this world is so flawed and filled with trouble! I could never survive if you were not protecting and guiding me. Thank you!

I am awed to think how much you care for me and all you do to protect me every day. Even in the midst of danger, you keep me safe with you. I ask for your protection today, Lord. Thank you for your armor. I put it all on. From my head to my feet, it covers me.

Help me use your Word and hold up my shield of faith today. Help me do the things that you have asked me to do. But keep me from trying to solve my problems the way the world solves problems. Keep me from relying on myself.

Even when my hopes crash around me, you are my safe place. I will wait for you to act. I praise you today because of who you are, my solid rock in every storm and my refuge always.

Amen.

Bless the LORD, O my soul,

and forget not all his benefits,

who forgives all your iniquity,

who heals all your diseases,

who redeems your life from the pit,

who crowns you with steadfast love and mercy,

who satisfies you with good

so that your youth is renewed like the eagle's. . . .

The LORD is merciful and gracious,

slow to anger and abounding in steadfast love. . . .

He does not deal with us according to our sins,

nor repay us according to our iniquities.

For as high as the heavens are above the earth,

so great is his steadfast love toward those who fear him;

as far as the east is from the west,

so far does he remove our transgressions from us.

PSALM 103:2–5, 8, 10–12

· VII ·
The Lord Is My Provider

David was furious. Nabal, a wealthy man in the region, had refused his request for supplies for himself and his men. After all that they had done for Nabal's shepherds! And on a feast day! How dare he?

Hiding from Saul in the wilderness of Paran near Carmel, David and his men had crossed paths many times with Nabal's sheep and shepherds. David and his men had treated them well, and at night their presence had provided protection for the shepherds against bandits and marauders who knew that coming anywhere near David's camp meant they would bear his justice.

David's request was customary, especially on a feast day, and not ill-founded. Seeing that Nabal had far more than enough and that he had protected his shepherds, David expected they would receive enough supplies to last for several months. Just the protection from raiders he had provided was worth far more than that. Nabal would never miss what David and his men so badly needed.

However, David had underestimated Nabal's harshness and greed. His request was refused, and the messengers he sent were shunned and insulted. It was the most unrighteous reply to a feast day request that David had ever heard of, and he was not in a mood to let it go unpunished. "Truly I have vainly guarded all that this fellow has in the wilderness," he said. "During this time he missed nothing, and for that he has returned me evil for good. So help me God if by morning I leave so much as one male alive in all his household." David decided he would pay Nabal a personal visit with four hundred of his armed men.

Along the way, however, they came across a caravan led by a beautiful woman heading their direction. When she saw David, she turned to meet him, climbed down from her donkey, and fell on her face before him. David was so shocked that for a moment he forgot his anger.

"On me alone, my lord, be the guilt," she said. "Please let your servant speak in your ears, and hear the words of your servant. Let not my lord regard this worthless fellow, Nabal.

"I, your servant, did not see your young men come to our house. My lord, as the LORD lives, and as your soul lives, God has restrained you from bloodguilt. Now let these gifts that your servant has brought to my lord be given to the young men who follow him." The small caravan following her carried two hundred loaves of bread, two skins of wine, five hundred sheep already butchered and preserved, five bags of parched grain, a hundred clusters of raisins, and two hundred fig cakes.

"Please forgive the trespass of your servant," the woman continued. "For God will certainly make my lord David a sure house, because you are fighting the battles of the Lord, and evil shall not be found in you so long as you live. If men rise up to pursue you and to seek your life, the life of my lord shall not be harmed because of the care of the Lord your God— while the lives of your enemies He shall fling out as from the hollow of His sling. And when God has done to my lord according to all the good that He has spoken concerning you and has appointed you prince over Israel, my lord shall have no cause of grief or pangs of conscience for having shed blood without cause or taking vengeance himself. I only ask that when God has dealt well with my lord, then you will remember your servant."

The woman's request struck David to the heart, and he knew she spoke righteously. So he granted her request and let her return unharmed to Nabal—who turned out to be her husband.

Nabal's guilt did not go unnoticed by the Lord, however, and because of his sin, Nabal died ten days later. When David heard this news, he praised God again that he had avoided the guilt he would have carried had he attacked Nabal's household. He sent messengers to find Abigail, Nabal's widow, who had come to him in her wisdom, which resulted in her household being spared as well as preventing David and his men from bloodguilt. And Abigail returned with his messengers and became David's wife. (See 1 Samuel 25 paraphrased.)

David had not exactly sought the Lord for provision, but God provided. David's prayer was for vengeance, and he was prepared to take it with his own hands. David was consumed by anger, but God was merciful. He sent Abigail to intercede with a bounty of supplies and a message of reason, providing David with an escape from the temptation to commit a grievous sin. And because David was receptive to the wisdom of God's grace and quick to turn his heart, God did indeed avenge David for Nabal's unrighteousness. Even more so, He blessed David with Abigail.

HELP WHEN NEEDED

God meets our needs in unsuspecting ways. What seems right and reasonable from our point of view may not at all be what God has in store. As we learn from Proverbs, "There is a way that seems right to a man, but its end is the way to death" (14:12). Nabal's way seemed right to him, but it brought about his death. What David and his men had set out to do seemed right in their eyes, but that also was the way of death.

God spared David because his heart was pure; David immediately responded to God's wisdom as spoken by Abigail because his heart was always sensitive to it. Think about what happened to Nabal when David let God act on his behalf as you read the following instruction from David:

Do not fret because of evil men
or be envious of those who do wrong;
for like the grass they will soon wither,
like green plants they will soon die away.
Trust in the LORD and do good;
dwell in the land and enjoy safe pasture.
Delight yourself in the LORD
and he will give you the desires of your heart. . . .
Be still before the LORD and wait patiently for him;
do not fret when men succeed in their ways,
when they carry out their wicked schemes.
Refrain from anger and turn from wrath;
do not fret—it leads only to evil.
For evil men will be cut off,
but those who hope in the LORD will inherit the land. . . .
I have seen a wicked and ruthless man
flourishing like a green tree in its native soil,
but he soon passed away and was no more;
though I looked for him, he could not be found.
PSALM 37:1-4, 7-9, 35-36 NIV

We know from Scripture that God always enriches the righteous—those whose faith is in God—and forsakes the wicked. If we can learn to trust the Lord and not lean on our own understanding, God will prepare a way for us regardless of our circumstances. (See Proverbs 3:4-6.) What better vindication than to be blessed by God before your foes? God will convict their hearts on your behalf. But the Lord requires one small but vital thing—your heart. God will fulfill your every need and heart's desire if you will fully trust Him.

> *Wait for the LORD and keep his way,*
> *and he will exalt you to inherit the land;*
> *you will look on when the wicked are cut off.*
> PSALM 37:34

What's more, when you commit your way to the Lord and trust Him, He will help you when you are not even expecting it. You might not have asked for God's help and neglected to place your problem squarely in His hands, but even when you stumble blindly on, He will bring you the light you need to see your answer.

> *If the LORD delights in a man's way,*
> *he makes his steps firm;*
> *though he stumble, he will not fall,*
> *for the LORD upholds him with his hand.*
> PSALM 37:23-24 NIV

What Do You Need?

We know our God is capable of meeting every conceivable need, but sometimes we think we can ask only so much from Him. After all, our cares seem endless; they are limitless! Should we pester Him with every little thing, or just go to Him with the bigger concerns that are more difficult for us to handle on our own? Should we go to the Lord only when we are desperate, or should we cast our every worry upon Him?

Going to the Lord with our every care can be challenging. For one, it requires a certain humility to continually knock on heaven's door for assistance. For another, it takes a certain amount of energy to turn our attention to God with every anxiety that rises up. But those moments of angst are the traps of the enemy. He uses them to attempt to win his subtle victories in our hearts and minds and separate us from God.

Trusting God for all things—at all times—takes discipline. We have to train our minds to meditate on God's willingness and ability to meet our every need. God is paying attention to how we respond to even the smallest concern. Read how Peter admonishes his readers in the following passage:

> Humble yourselves, therefore, under the mighty hand of God
> so that at the proper time he may exalt you, casting all your
> anxieties on him, because he cares for you. Be sober-minded;

> be watchful. Your adversary the devil prowls around like a
> roaring lion, seeking someone to devour.
> 1 PETER 5:6-8

No matter what your need, big or small, God not only cares for you, He is watching for an opportunity to move through your faith as you lean on and trust in Him. There is no worry that is too insignificant and no problem too huge that God cannot take care of it. As David reminded himself often, God created the heavens and the stars, the earth and seas, and everything that lives, yet He is mindful of man:

> When I look at your heavens, the work of your fingers,
> the moon and the stars, which you have set in place,
> what is man that you are mindful of him,
> and the son of man that you care for him?
> PSALM 8:3-4

David sang often of the glory and majesty of all God created. He continually reminded himself of all God was capable of. It is difficult for our human brains to comprehend God's capacity to love, so David continually reminded himself of the faithfulness and goodness of God. Doing so with a grateful heart was central to David's success. David did just that when he composed the following psalm to God:

The eyes of all look to you,
and you give them their food in due season.
You open your hand;
you satisfy the desire of every living thing.
The LORD is righteous in all his ways
and kind in all his works.
The LORD is near to all who call on him,
to all who call on him in truth.
He fulfills the desire of those who fear him;
he also hears their cry and saves them.
The LORD preserves all who love him,
but all the wicked he will destroy.
PSALM 145:15-20

We too can remind ourselves of God's willingness and power to provide all of our needs.

I have been young, and now am old,
yet I have not seen the righteous forsaken
or his children begging for bread.
PSALM 37:25

Father God,

Why is it so hard for me to trust you to provide for me? Is it because I stay so busy providing for myself that I get to feeling that I can handle it all? Help me to realize that even my abilities and my employment come from you!

And then there are the times when I become aware that I can't handle it—when a disaster hits or the job runs out or my health breaks down. Then I turn to you for help. But when the crisis is over, sometimes I forget.

Forgive me for my foolishness. Forgive me for forgetting that you are always my provider. No matter what my circumstances, you have promised to provide and care for me, and you always do what you say.

Help me train my mind to rely on you alone each day. Teach me to discipline myself to come to you with the smallest concern. Help me grasp that you are indeed a Father who delights in giving good gifts to His children. Keep me from pridefully depending on myself!

You clothe the lilies, see the smallest sparrow, and call all the stars by name. Whatever it is that I need today, I ask you to provide. Remind me today that I have no need you cannot meet. Thank you for loving me and caring for me so completely and perfectly.

Amen.

You have tried my heart, you have visited me by night,
you have tested me, and you will find nothing;
I have purposed that my mouth will not transgress.
With regard to the works of man, by the word of your lips
I have avoided the ways of the violent.
My steps have held fast to your paths;
my feet have not slipped.
I call upon you, for you will answer me, O God;
incline your ear to me; hear my words.
Wondrously show your steadfast love,
O Savior of those who seek refuge
from their adversaries at your right hand.
Keep me as the apple of your eye;
hide me in the shadow of your wings,
from the wicked who do me violence,
my deadly enemies who surround me. . . .
Arise, O Lord! Confront him, subdue him!
Deliver my soul from the wicked by your sword,
from men by your hand, O Lord,
from men of the world whose portion is in this life.
You fill their womb with treasure;
they are satisfied with children,
and they leave their abundance to their infants.
As for me, I shall behold your face in righteousness;
when I awake, I shall be satisfied with your likeness.

Psalm 17:3–9, 13–15

· VIII ·
The Lord Is My Reward

After years of wandering as an outlaw, David established a camp at Ziklag for his army and the families of his men. It was there that word came to David that Saul and Jonathan had been killed in battle.

David tore his robes in sorrow after hearing of the death of his enemy, the king of Israel, and his friend the prince. Later on, after a period of mourning, David inquired of the Lord what he should do next, and the Lord told him to go to Hebron. There he was anointed king over the tribe of Judah.

While David reigned over Judah, Ish-bosheth, another son of Saul, reigned over the rest of Israel in Jerusalem. There was never peace between the soldiers on either side. After two years, Ish-bosheth was killed by his own captains, who hoped to ingratiate themselves to David. But David had them executed instead, declaring, "As the LORD lives, . . . when wicked men have killed a righteous man in his own house on his bed, shall I not now require his blood at your hand and destroy you from the earth?" (2 Samuel 4:9,11).

Despite the feud, however, the people of Israel saw that David was an honest man who had not incited any of the violence toward the house of Saul. As a result, the elders of Israel went to David and asked him to be their king as well: "Behold, we are your bone and flesh. In times past, when Saul was king over us, it was you who led out and brought in Israel. And the LORD said to you, 'You shall be shepherd of my people Israel, and you shall be prince over Israel'" (2 Samuel 5:1-2).

At their request, David agreed to be anointed king of Israel in Hebron. He was thirty-two years old. Finally, what Samuel had anointed him for as a young man more than a decade earlier, had become a reality—even though David had never taken it upon himself to try to win the throne of Israel in the place of Saul. In gratitude, David prayed:

> Who am I, O Lord GOD, and what is my house, that you
> have brought me thus far? And yet this was a small thing in

your eyes, O Lord GOD. You have spoken also of your servant's house for a great while to come, and this is instruction for mankind, O Lord GOD! And what more can David say to you?

For you know your servant, O Lord GOD! Because of your promise, and according to your own heart, you have brought about all this greatness, to make your servant know it. Therefore you are great, O LORD God. For there is none like you, and there is no God besides you, according to all that we have heard with our ears. . . .

And now, O LORD God, confirm forever the word that you have spoken concerning your servant and concerning his house, and do as you have spoken. And your name will be magnified forever, saying, "The LORD of hosts is God over Israel," and the house of your servant David will be established before you. For you, O LORD of hosts, the God of Israel, have made this revelation to your servant, saying, "I will build you a house." Therefore your servant has found courage to pray this prayer to you.

And now, O Lord GOD, you are God, and your words are true, and you have promised this good thing to your servant. Now therefore may it please you to bless the house of your servant, so that it may continue forever before you. For you, O

Lord GOD, have spoken, and with your blessing shall the house of your servant be blessed forever.

2 SAMUEL 7:18-22, 25-29

(PARAGRAPH BREAKS ADDED)

David's struggles were not in vain. Through years of service as a shepherd, a court bard, and a captain of armies, he learned to have the heart of a servant. Through years of living as an outlaw, he learned to cling to God and follow His ways no matter what the short-term cost. He also learned firsthand what a king should not be and what the abuse of power could cost a nation.

> DAVID WAS NEVER IN THE PURSUIT OF THE THRONE ... DAVID MADE THE CHOICE TO PURSUE GOD.

What held David through it all? He knew he had a hope and a future in the Lord. David was never in the pursuit of the throne—even though that is what God ultimately had for him. Instead, David made the choice to pursue God.

THE PLACE OF REWARD

While David did embrace his role as a leader and a soldier, this never distracted him from fulfilling what he considered to be his primary purpose—seeking God with all his heart.

> You have said, "Seek my face."
> My heart says to you,
> "Your face, LORD, do I seek."
> Psalm 27:8

David never confused seeking God's hand—how God can bless us—with seeking God's face—how we know Him and enter His presence. He knew there was more joy to be found simply by basking in God's presence than he could find anywhere else.

> There are many who say, "Who will show us some good?
> Lift up the light of your face upon us, O LORD!"
> You have put more joy in my heart
> than they have when their grain and wine abound.
> PSALM 4:6-7

Unfortunately, many of David's mistakes happened when he paid more attention to trusting in his blessings rather than seeking to please his Lord. But for much of his life, God was not a means to get what he wanted, but the object of his desire itself. From David's perspective, God was never his rewarder as much as his reward.

THE ART OF SEEKING GOD

One thing that marked David's life was a sense of quietness and waiting—much more than most of us experience today. Imagine for a moment what it must have been like to be a shepherd. Not just hours of leading a flock from one pasture and stream to another, but weeks, days, and months of it! How many hours a day did David just sit around watching his sheep eat? As a military man, he must have spent days upon days marching to the next battlefield, setting up camp, and waiting for the next conflict. As a fugitive, he must have had long evenings to wonder where Saul was and how he might be planning to trap him next.

> ONE THING THAT MARKED DAVID'S LIFE WAS A SENSE OF QUIETNESS AND WAITING.

Yet it seems unlikely that David let these hours pass on such wasted worries. Instead he took the time to play his lyre, sing his prayers, and write his psalms. And David didn't have the option of creating habits connected to any particular places either. He didn't have a favorite chair that was the only place he felt comfortable reading God's law or a quiet, private "prayer closet" where he could open his heart to the Lord. For years David didn't know where he would be from one day to the next. All he ever had was the moment. The fulfillment of God's plan for his life may have never come to pass had he thought, *Well, when I finally get this situation with Saul resolved, then I will have time to read God's Word and sing His praises on a regular basis.*

Realize that wherever you are at any moment is a time and place where you can let praises to God absorb your heart. You can meditate on the portion of the Bible you read this morning and let the Holy Spirit give you new insight about it. Every moment is an opportunity to take whatever concern is causing you anxiety and lay it before the Lord. If we will pursue the presence of God with half the vigor we have for pursuing distraction and entertainment, we will experience revival unlike anything we have ever known.

> EVERY MOMENT IS AN OPPORTUNITY TO TAKE WHATEVER CONCERN IS CAUSING YOU ANXIETY AND LAY IT BEFORE THE LORD.

Jesus expressed it this way: "The kingdom of heaven is like a treasure hidden in a field, which a man found and covered up. Then in his joy he goes and sells all that he has and buys that field. Again, the kingdom of heaven is like a merchant in search of fine pearls, who, on finding one pearl of great value, went and sold all that he had and bought it" (Matthew 13:44-46).

The treasure seeker and the merchant in these parables knew what was important and what wasn't. They chose to give up everything they had in order to win the one thing of greatest value, and that is God himself! David understood this principle. Although he had opportunities to kill King Saul and "have it all"—the kingdom, riches, and power—he pursued God alone rather than pursue ambition. God became his prize!

Even when David's sin with Bathsheba was revealed, his greatest concern was the possibility that God might withdraw from him. He pleaded with God:

> Do not cast me from your presence
> or take your Holy Spirit from me.
> PSALM 51:11 NIV

Perhaps one of the most important lessons for our day is that we, too, can know God as intimately as David did. David wasn't born with a special "knowing God" gene that allowed him special access into God's presence. He simply hungered for God and refused to let anything satisfy that hunger except God himself. Even when times were rough, David again and again proved that God was all that mattered to him. Even if following God meant living in a cave or on the run, David allowed God to bring about His perfect plan for his life.

God is not as interested in what we *have* as in what has *us*. To follow in David's footsteps toward knowing God doesn't necessarily mean we are to give up everything we have. However, if everything we have keeps us from wholeheartedly pursuing God, we will be the ones to suffer loss. We will not have the kind of relationship with God that David had.

> PURSUING GOD HAS LESS TO DO WITH WHAT WE GIVE UP AND MORE TO DO WITH MAKING HIM A PRIORITY.

Pursuing God has less to do with what we give up and more to do with making Him a priority. Probably more than for any other generation that has lived, ours is an age of distractions. Getting to know God truly takes concentrated effort and time. As you meditate on David's prayers, make a decision to put God first on your list today. Spend some time reading His Word and seeking His presence. You will not be disappointed! God himself says:

> *You will seek me and find me when you seek me with all*
> *your heart.*
> JEREMIAH 29:13 NIV

You may be thinking, *What does seeking God mean?* First of all, it begins with an attitude of the heart. We must realize our desperate need of Him. Sometimes life goes smoothly without a hitch, and we can become complacent in our relationship to God. Then come the hard times—the death of a loved one, a divorce, a job loss—and suddenly we're not so invincible. But we need to keep that attitude of desperation for God through good times and bad times. We always need Him whether we realize it or not!

Second, seeking God means making Him a priority. That may mean getting up early to spend time in prayer and Bible study. It may mean turning off the television. Whatever it means to you, it will require your commitment and the investment of your time and life. But remember—your reward will be God himself! There is no one or nothing that could be better.

Heavenly Father,

Sometimes I wonder if my struggles are worth it. Life seems so unfair at times. My circumstances change from bad to worse.

And then, somehow, I get to the other side of things. When I look back, I can see how you were working in my struggle, and I have a new experience of you to share with others.

Or, my situation doesn't change, but somehow I am changed. In the midst of my trouble, I know that you are with me, and I have peace.

Increase my hunger for you, God! When I am tempted to put off spending time with you until my life is better, remind me how unwise that is. Help me make getting to know you my priority, no matter what kind of day it is, because you always reward those who seek you. You reward us with yourself. And that, more than anything else, is what I really want.

Amen.

O God, you are my God; earnestly I seek you;

my soul thirsts for you;

my flesh faints for you,

as in a dry and weary land where there is no water.

So I have looked upon you in the sanctuary,

beholding your power and glory.

Because your steadfast love is better than life,

my lips will praise you.

So I will bless you as long as I live;

in your name I will lift up my hands.

My soul will be satisfied as with fat and rich food,

and my mouth will praise you with joyful lips,

when I remember you upon my bed,

and meditate on you in the watches of the night;

for you have been my help,

and in the shadow of your wings I will sing for joy.

My soul clings to you;

your right hand upholds me.

PSALM 63:1–8

· IX ·
THE LORD IS MY PASSION

Michal stared from her window in contempt. *The desert has made David common!* she thought. *He is a fool! Look at how he is dressed!*

David wore a linen tunic as if he were a simple priest, not a king! Where were his robes of state? Michal thought David should be riding high above the people, but instead he was parading before them—even before servant girls! It was indecent. He was leaping and dancing in the streets!

Michal continued watching the procession from her palace window. That golden box the priests were carrying between them on poles must be the Ark of the Covenant.

She had never seen it before. How it gleamed in the sunlight! Finally it was returning to its rightful place—to Jerusalem, the capital of this great nation! But not like this; it shouldn't be brought back like this!

Michal looked again at her husband celebrating with the commoners, dancing with girls playing tambourines, and shouting with the cheering crowds. Her husband! David had left her behind when he escaped the palace and fled from Saul, and Saul had given Michal to Paltiel, the son of Laish. He wasn't as handsome or daring as David, but he loved her. She wasn't sure why David had ordered that she be given back to him when her father died. Did he love her? He had other wives now besides Michal, and they had given him children.

Her disgust increased. Where was David's dignity? How could God have picked this man to be king instead of her father? It seemed it was up to her to teach him to stand in his station and demand the respect and admiration—the fear—due the king of the great nation of Israel.

"Rebecca! Anna!" she called. "We will meet the king when he enters the palace. Bring my finest robe!"

The two servant girls felt the sting in their mistress's voice and obeyed quickly. When they had her ready to meet her lord, Michal rose up to her full height, straightened her back and held her head erect, and walked slowly, with great dignity, to the throne room. The two servant girls followed quietly.

David stood in the hall greeting friends and family with great enthusiasm. Then he called to all present, "This is a great day, my brothers! The Ark of the Lord has returned to Jerusalem! The glorious God of our fathers—the God of Abraham, Isaac, and Jacob—has smiled upon us again! His mercy endures forever! Give thanks to the God of heaven!"

But as Michal entered the chamber, everyone grew quiet. David turned to greet her warmly but stopped suddenly when he saw her expression. She looked him over from head to foot slowly, so that he could see her disdain. He still wore the tunic of a simple priest. It was as if he were dressed only in his undergarments! She smiled coldly. "How glorious the king of Israel looked today! He exposed himself to the servant girls like an indecent person might do!"

David's face was like steel. He didn't move, but it seemed he rose up ten feet tall. His words carried an authority he had never used with her before. "I was dancing before the Lord—He who appointed me as the leader of Israel, His people! Yes, I am willing to act like a fool in order to show my joy before Him." Though she fought it, a shiver rolled down Michal's spine. "Yes, I am willing to look even more foolish than this," David continued. "But I will be held in honor by the girls of whom you have spoken, not contempt, because this day I glorified the Lord."

The room grew even quieter. Michal, the daughter of Saul, the wife of David, felt her knees go weak beneath her, but her contempt remained. She bowed her head with as much grace as her lack of composure could muster, turned on her heels, and returned to her chamber. Halfway up the stairs, she heard the roar of praise return to the throne room. She halfheartedly looked back and noticed Rebecca and Anna were no longer following her. She started to call them, but caught herself. *Let them stay,* she thought. *If it is the honor of servant girls he wants, then that is all he shall get!*

Michal's contempt would cost her greatly—she remained childless to the day of her death. (See 2 Samuel 6:12-23.)

What made David an extraordinary shepherd, warrior, and king? It was the condition of his heart. God promoted David, protected him, and propelled him to victory because his heart was soft for the Lord; he was a man after God's own heart. (See 1 Samuel 13:14.) David was transparent before his Creator and hungry for more of His Spirit. David searched deeply within himself and turned his heart inside out before the Lord.

> O Lord, all my longing is before you;
> my sighing is not hidden from you. . . .
> But for you, O LORD, do I wait;
> it is you, O Lord my God, who will answer.
> PSALM 38:9, 15

WHAT ARE YOU PASSIONATELY PURSUING?

David followed God's lead. He learned to be passionate because his Creator was passionate. From the beauty around him, David saw that the master of the universe had spared nothing when it came to His creation. No detail was too great or too small for Him to care for. From the sheer vastness of the sky above to the detail of each flower below, God's handiwork moved David's heart. He pondered God's workmanship and saw the majesty and glory of

God in all He had set His hand to. It compelled him to pen, "The heavens declare the glory of God . . ." (Psalm 19:1 NIV).

David saw God's fingerprints on all of creation. He understood that we, as created beings, are a reflection of God—and more, how right it is that the passion and intensity with which God created us should be reflected back to Him. David grasped the depth of God's enthusiasm as Creator; God enjoyed His creation so much that David could not help but be thrilled by his Creator.

> On the glorious splendor of your majesty,
> and on your wondrous works, I will meditate.
> Psalm 145:5

> I will give thanks to the LORD with my whole heart;
> I will recount all of your wonderful deeds.
> I will be glad and exult in you;
> I will sing praise to your name, O Most High.
> Psalm 9:1-2

David was the first writer of Scripture to really carry on about how blessed we are that God loves us—those who are on the receiving end of God's infinite love and boundless passion.

> Blessed are the people to whom such blessings fall!

> *Blessed are the people whose God is the LORD!*
> PSALM 144:15

David knew that no matter how much we love or give or lay down our lives, we cannot come close to God's capacity to love, give, and sacrifice for the sake of those He loves. With all his heart, mind, and strength, David tried to return the love he felt God pouring out upon him. "Let Your mercy and loving-kindness, O Lord, be upon us, in proportion to our waiting and hoping for You" (Psalm 33:22 AMP).

LIVING FROM THE HEART

As a boy, as David watched over his father's flocks, he had many opportunities to reflect and meditate on the greatness of God. He must have learned not only to hear the voice of God but also the voice of his own heart responding to God. As a youth, he must have learned to pay attention to his heart's yearnings and convictions. It was from the wellspring of his heart that David composed and sang songs to the Lord, a wellspring flowing with gratitude and awe for the God who had made His

IT WAS FROM THE WELLSPRING OF HIS HEART THAT DAVID COMPOSED AND SANG SONGS TO THE LORD.

presence known—a God David could hear and feel in the depths of his heart.

From the depths of this well flowed David's passion for God. He lived from his heart—a heart humbled by the majesty of God and moved by the love of a heavenly Father. The fullness of God's presence compelled him to sing, to dance, to give glory to God. He understood that the longing in his heart was both given and fulfilled by this wonder-working God—and the more David delighted in Him, the more desirous he became for Him.

> Delight yourself also in the LORD,
> And He shall give you the desires of your heart.
> PSALM 37:4 NKJV

As God filled his heart, David was able to articulate and act upon the longings and desires residing deep within him. For David, a huge part of that was seeing God glorified and celebrated. How fervently did he cry out to God as he sat alone playing his lyre, meditating on God's faithfulness, worshiping, and composing songs of praise? How much more determined was he to put into words what was bursting inside of him about God's greatness, goodness, and love?

In those still places where we are quiet and able to wait on the Lord, if we are willing to honestly open ourselves up to Him, we too will come face-to-face with our own heart's desire to know God more fully and make Him more fully known. We will discover what David did—that it is the pursuit of God that gives meaning to every other pursuit.

> ... IF WE ARE WILLING TO HONESTLY OPEN OURSELVES UP TO HIM, WE TOO WILL COME FACE-TO-FACE WITH OUR OWN HEART'S DESIRE TO KNOW GOD MORE FULLY.

UNDERSTANDING DAVID'S PASSION

When we come to that place where we are consumed, as David was, by a desire for more of God, we will find the passion and fullness of joy that can be experienced only in God's presence. When God becomes the object of your passion—when He increasingly becomes the desire of your heart as you delight in Him—then you will discover joy indescribable.

> *You will show me the path of life;*
> *In Your presence is fullness of joy;*
> *At Your right hand are pleasures forevermore.*
> PSALM 16:11 NKJV

And once you've experienced that joy, nothing will keep you from it. A passion such as David's is ever joyful. He delighted in the Lord and could not say enough about the importance of rejoicing before Him. When there is such joy, there can be no shame. And that was one of the hallmarks of David's passion: it was shameless. He danced unashamedly before the Lord regardless of what others thought. He remembered what the Lord had done for him, and it humbled him. His passion left no room for pride. He reminded himself continually of all the Lord had done, and he rejoiced without restraint.

No matter where he was or who he was with, he would praise the Lord. Not only was David Israel's greatest king, but he was the kingdom's greatest worshiper. More than anything, what made him history's most passionate worshiper was that he believed with his whole heart all he declared. With every fiber of his being he believed every inspired Scripture he read and he placed his entire hope in God:

> I will bless the LORD at all times;
> his praise shall continually be in my mouth.
> My soul makes its boast in the LORD;
> let the humble hear and be glad.
> Oh, magnify the LORD with me,
> and let us exalt his name together!
> I sought the LORD, and he answered me
> and delivered me from all my fears.

Those who look to him are radiant,
and their faces shall never be ashamed.
PSALM 34:1-5

David had personally experienced God as his king, friend, provider, and refuge; he experienced firsthand God's salvation, joy, and reward—all of which continually fed David's passionate zeal for glorifying God. He had walked through many troubles with the Lord by his side, and the Lord had proven His faithfulness time and again. David made it a point never to forget. He stirred up his gratitude by remembering God's goodness at every opportunity:

I remember the days of old;
I meditate on all that you have done;
I ponder the work of your hands.
I stretch out my hands to you;
my soul thirsts for you like a parched land.
    Selah
PSALM 143:5-6

David laid it all down. He made known to the multitudes where his priorities were—whom he served and what he lived, fought, and strived for. He wasn't conservative or reserved in that respect. There was but one thing that motivated him, one thing that drove him—and that was to drink more deeply of the goodness of God every day of his life.

> *One thing have I asked of the LORD,*
> *that will I seek after:*
> *that I may dwell in the house of the LORD*
> *all the days of my life,*
> *to gaze upon the beauty of the LORD*
> *and to inquire in his temple.*
> PSALM 27:4

Father God,

I long to be wholehearted toward you, as David was. He recognized your passion for your creation and for your children, and he wasn't afraid to reflect that same love and passion back to you. Please help me learn to live like that.

Help me always to be aware that my abilities and gifts are from you, and show me how to dedicate my creativity to you. Guide me as I develop and use my talents. Help me be true to the person you created me to be and to live every day from my heart.

May I praise you always, in all things. May I never be ashamed to let my love for you be known—to speak a word about you when someone needs to hear it, and never to hold back.

Even in my most lonely, angry, worried times, Lord, help me be as honest with you as David was. And after I have vented my frustration and fear, let me praise you again, just like he did.

May my passion always be for you and your ways, and may I have the joy of knowing you all the days of my life.

Amen.

Have mercy on me, O God,
according to your steadfast love;
according to your abundant mercy
blot out my transgressions.
Wash me thoroughly from my iniquity,
and cleanse me from my sin!
For I know my transgressions,
and my sin is ever before me.
Against you, you only, have I sinned
and done what is evil in your sight,
so that you may be justified in your words
and blameless in your judgment. . . .
Create in me a clean heart, O God,
and renew a right spirit within me.
Cast me not away from your presence,
and take not your Holy Spirit from me.
Restore to me the joy of your salvation,
and uphold me with a willing spirit.
Then I will teach transgressors your ways,
and sinners will return to you.
Deliver me from bloodguiltiness, O God,
O God of my salvation,
and my tongue will sing aloud of your righteousness.
O Lord, open my lips,
and my mouth will declare your praise.
For you will not delight in sacrifice, or I would give it;
you will not be pleased with a burnt offering.
The sacrifices of God are a broken spirit;
a broken and contrite heart, O God, you will not despise.

PSALM 51:1–4, 10–17

· X ·
THE LORD IS MY FORGIVENESS

Nathan the prophet went to David quietly and inauspiciously. He had requested a private audience and David had granted it. Upon exchanging formal greetings, Nathan laid his question before the king.

"In a certain village near here, there were two men. One was rich, and the other was poor. The rich man had a great wealth of flocks and herds, while the poor man had nothing but one little ewe, which he raised as if it were his own child among his other children. He fed it from his own plate and let it drink from his own cup. At night, it slept on his breast. It was like a daughter to him.

"Then a traveler came to the rich man, but he refused to take a lamb from his own flocks to feed the traveler. Instead he took the poor man's lamb and prepared it as a meal for his guest."

David's anger rose within him at the injustice. "As God in heaven lives, this rich man deserves to die for his lack of pity! He must restore the lamb fourfold because he did this thing."

For the first time Nathan looked up and met David's eyes. "You are the rich man!"

The words stung, and David looked at him in utter amazement. His heart fell limp within him. A sense of panic gripped him at the thought that he could commit such an act, and he wanted to tell Nathan he was mistaken, yet somehow he could not. A hidden guilt he had been ignoring rose up from his stomach, and he found nothing to say to Nathan in response.

Nathan's gaze had not wandered in the meantime. "Thus says the Lord, the God of Israel, 'I anointed you king over my people Israel and kept you safe as Saul pursued your life. I have given you his house and his wives and all that you could desire from the houses of Judah and Israel. And if these were too little for you, had you asked, I would have given you more. Yet instead you despised my word and performed this great act of selfishness and evil. You had Uriah the Hittite murdered and took his wife as your own. Therefore the sword shall not depart from your house, and you shall suffer at the hands of your own children.'"

David's blood ran cold. He had been so careful to keep all of this hidden, but how could he be so foolish as to think he could hide a thing from God? How had he let himself embark on such a path of treachery and self-deception? Had he really believed he could cover all this up?

For a moment, a voice in the back of his mind suggested that if he had Nathan killed, no one else would know. Or perhaps he could plead with Nathan to forgive him, and between the two of them they could work something out. Was there not some way he could justify himself before Nathan—something he could say to smooth this thing out?

Yet where shall I go from God's Spirit? he thought. *What hope do I have of escaping from His presence? There is no darkness He cannot see through. I cannot escape His righteousness— and why would I want to? Wouldn't I trade all that I have to be once more in His grace? What great foolishness have I allowed to lead me down this path? Even if it means my death, I have nowhere else to go besides back to God.*

Fully prepared to accept God's judgment upon himself even as he had declared judgment on the rich man in Nathan's story, David looked at Nathan and said, "I have sinned against the Lord."

Nathan saw the king's regret at what he had done, and the Spirit of God again spoke within Nathan's spirit. "The Lord has put away your sin and you will not die," Nathan told David, "but because of the scorn you have shown the Lord, the fruit of your adultery with Uriah's wife—the child shall not live."

Nathan turned and left the room.

David tore his robes and fell to the ground. When he heard that the child was sick, he fasted and lay prostrate all the night, pleading with God for the child's life. For seven days he stayed like this; none of his advisors could persuade him to get up or eat. On the seventh day, the child died. David's servants were afraid to tell him, but from their demeanor he surmised that this was so, and he asked, "Is the child dead?"

When he heard that it was so, he rose, washed, changed his garments, and went to the tabernacle and worshiped. (See 2 Samuel 12:1-20.)

Unlike Saul, when David was confronted by God's prophet regarding a transgression, David turned to God for forgiveness. Unlike Saul, he didn't make excuses or plead with the prophet to show him pity; David deeply felt the shame of what he had done:

> Have mercy on me, O God,
> according to your unfailing love;
> according to your great compassion
> blot out my transgressions.
> Wash away all my iniquity
> and cleanse me from my sin.
> PSALM 51:1-2 NIV

"CAST ME NOT AWAY FROM YOUR PRESENCE"

As David continued to seek the Lord for restoration, he begged God not to cast him away from His presence (Psalm 51:11). Anything else he could bear, but not life outside of God's loving embrace. In God's presence David found the grace he sought. He would not find compassion, mercy, or peace anywhere except in the presence of his heavenly Father. Where else could he turn?

> Create in me a pure heart, O God,
> and renew a steadfast spirit within me. . . .

> *Restore to me the joy of your salvation*
> *and grant me a willing spirit, to sustain me.*
> PSALM 51:10, 12 NIV

While man has a tendency to seek justice, David knew God would be merciful. Listen to David's words in 2 Samuel 24:14: "Let us fall into the hand of the LORD, for his mercy is great; but let me not fall into the hand of man." Only God could show the depth of compassion David needed.

Sometimes we need to be rescued from ourselves as much as from our enemies. When we can't live with our own selves for the shame and guilt of our mistakes, there is only One we can turn to for consolation. We know there is no thought or intent hidden from God. Our only answer lies in humbling ourselves before Him.

> *The LORD is gracious and compassionate,*
> *slow to anger and rich in love.*
> *The LORD is good to all;*
> *he has compassion on all he has made. . . .*
> *The LORD upholds all those who fall*
> *and lifts up all who are bowed down. . . .*
> *The LORD is near to all who call on him,*
> *to all who call on him in truth.*
> *He fulfills the desires of those who fear him;*

he hears their cry and saves them.
PSALM 145:8-9, 14, 18-19 NIV

BEAUTY FOR ASHES

Although he did everything within his power to intercede for the life of his baby, once the child died David immediately went to the tabernacle to worship. In God's presence, David found love, acceptance, and forgiveness even though he had sinned. God met him there and "renewed a right spirit" within him. David sought the Lord, throwing himself into God's arms, and the Lord caught him.

His sin behind him, David found the restoration he sought and the forgiveness he sorely needed. He was able to continue in the grace of God, resume his duties as God's anointed king, and go on to father Israel's wisest leader. The next son born to David and Bathsheba was none other than Solomon.

You have turned for me my mourning into dancing;
you have loosed my sackcloth
and clothed me with gladness,
that my glory may sing your praise and not be silent.
O LORD my God, I will give thanks to you forever!
PSALM 30:11-12

Turning our "mourning into dancing" is God's specialty.

God will turn every bad situation we get ourselves into, toward our good, if we will repent and turn to Him for restoration.

There are many examples of this in Scripture. One of the most notable is shown in the life of Solomon. Even though David's sin resulted in the death of his and Bathsheba's first child, God mercifully allowed them to have a second son who would actually become a part of Christ's ancestral line. Solomon would also have the distinguishing characteristic of being the wisest man who ever lived, and God even entrusted him with the building of the temple in which the Lord's presence would dwell. David's repentance and restoration paved the pathway for God to bring these blessings upon David and Bathsheba.

Another example is shown in the life of Rahab. (See Joshua 2.) She was a prostitute in a foreign nation. When some Israelites came into her land to spy it out for military purposes, she hid them from the authorities. Her explanation for doing this was that she knew the Israelites were going to be victorious and she knew that their God was the one true God! God had obviously revealed himself to her and she obviously repented and turned to God for her salvation. After hiding the men, she asked them to spare her and her family when they came back to invade her nation. Not only was she spared, but she actually became a part of Christ's ancestry also. She became David's great-great-grandmother!

Likewise, God showed David mercy after his great sin, enabling David to have a fresh start. David continued to pursue God with his whole heart. Deep within himself, he was convinced of the mercy and faithfulness of God. How could God deny himself and His covenant relationship with David?

The Lord had proven himself to David over years of seemingly insurmountable challenges and difficulties. God was with him as he battled an angry giant and jealous kings; the Lord provided as he struggled to survive as an outcast in the desert; God healed his heart after it had been broken by those he loved; and God sustained him when he was alone and confused. But most important of all, God forgave him when he stumbled and fell prey to his own humanity.

> RATHER THAN RUN FROM GOD WHEN HE FAILED, HE UNRESERVEDLY RAN TOWARD GOD IN FULL CONFIDENCE THAT REDEMPTION WOULD BE FOUND ONLY IN HIM.

David was a great and glorious king, a warrior, a poet, and a musician, but he was as fallible as anyone else. What set him apart was his willingness to repent.

His heart would not be moved in that regard. Rather than run from God when he failed, he unreservedly ran toward God in full confidence that redemption could be found only in Him. David had learned long before that the only place he longed to be and needed to be was in the presence of the One who loved him most.

> I will be glad and rejoice in your love,
> for you saw my affliction
> and knew the anguish of my soul.
> You have not handed me over to the enemy
> but have set my feet in a spacious place.
> PSALM 31:7-8 NIV

Father God,

Your forgiveness is a blessing that I do not deserve. Thank you, Jesus, for dying for me to secure my pardon forever. How can I thank you, God, for all that you have done for me?

May I not dwell on my mistakes. Help me confess them to you and to others that I may be healed. Show me what I need to learn from my sins and failures, and then help me move beyond them, praising you.

Thank you that I can come to you boldly because of Jesus' sacrifice for me. Allow me the privilege of helping to spread the message of your forgiveness to others today.

Help me, Lord, to see myself as you now see me—forgiven, cleansed, and free. Teach me to use my freedom to love and serve you every day. Help me always to choose your ways and not my own.

Thank you for being my forgiveness.

Amen.

I will sing of your love and justice;
to you, O LORD, I will sing praise.
I will be careful to lead a blameless life—
when will you come to me?
I will walk in my house
with blameless heart.
I will set before my eyes
no vile thing.
The deeds of faithless men I hate;
they will not cling to me.
Men of perverse heart shall be far from me;
I will have nothing to do with evil.
Whoever slanders his neighbor in secret,
him will I put to silence;
whoever has haughty eyes and a proud heart,
him will I not endure.
My eyes will be on the faithful in the land,
that they may dwell with me;
he whose walk is blameless
will minister to me.

PSALM 101:1-6 NIV

⧫ XI ⧫
DAVID'S PRAYER OF
COMMITMENT

D avid sat on his throne wondering at all that God had
done in his life. There was peace in the nation of
Israel, and the country was prospering. His government
was set in place to speak to the needs of God's people, and
honest courts had been established to ensure that God's
justice reigned over raiding armies and corruption. For the
first time in his rule, he did not feel overwhelmed by the
responsibilities of leadership. God had given him good
men to work with, and he was now free to reflect on other
things. As he did, he remembered Jonathan and his
covenant with him.

He summoned his advisors and asked, "Is there anyone left from the house of Saul to whom I might show kindness in remembrance of my friend and brother, Jonathan? Send out messengers to search for the servants of Saul who still live, to see if there is anyone left of Jonathan's house that I might bless."

David's advisors did as instructed, and a servant of Saul's named Ziba was found and brought to David. When David put his question to Ziba, he was told that the son of Jonathan, named Mephibosheth, was still alive and lived in Lo-debar. He also learned that Mephibosheth had been crippled as a child; in the confusion that ensued at the palace after Saul and Jonathan were killed at the battle of Jezreel, a nurse carrying Mephibosheth fell as she fled with him. David sent a troop of men to bring Mephibosheth to him. When Mephibosheth came before David, he fell face down to the floor. "I am your servant," he said.

David asked that Mephibosheth be raised to his feet. He saw fear in his eyes and wondered what Mephibosheth might have been told about him as he was growing up.

"Don't be afraid. I haven't called you here to hurt you but to bless you for your father's sake. He and I were very close. In memory of your father Jonathan, I want to restore to you all of the lands and houses of your grandfather Saul. All of his land will be yours, as well as all that belonged to his house. You shall also always have a place at my table and are welcome to eat with me at every meal."

Mephibosheth bowed again, "What is your servant that you should regard him as more than the dead dog he is?"

"You are the son of my friend Jonathan, and therefore my friend as well. For the sake of my promises to him, you will never be in need of anything ever again if it is in my power to provide it for you. You shall be as one of my sons, and I shall be like a father to you since your father is dead."

Mephibosheth looked up into the king's eyes and could see he was not being mocked. This man he had learned to fear and hide from all of his life was nothing like he expected. "Blessed, then, be the friend of my father. I will forever be grateful for your mercy on me and my father's house. Praises be to God that such a righteous man sits on the throne of Israel!" (See 2 Samuel 9.)

David understood the word commitment—he lived it! He had made a covenant with Jonathan and now at last he could celebrate his covenant with Jonathan and make good on his promise. David had watched God keep His word to him time and time again. Now David had an opportunity to show that same commitment by keeping his word to another.

A MAN OF HIS WORD

Not only did David keep his word, he also watched over his words—being careful to speak words pleasing to the Lord. In Psalm 19:14, he prayed that the words of his mouth and the meditation of his heart would always be acceptable to God. His dedication to God was so strong that he didn't want to offend Him in either words or actions. Obviously, our words are important to God because a great deal is said about them throughout the letters of Paul, Peter, and James. James went as far as to write, "For we all stumble in many things. If anyone does not stumble in word, he is a perfect man, able also to bridle the whole body" (James 3:2 NKJV).

Keeping his word and making sure that his words reflected his devotion to God required discipline on David's part. He was diligent in what some would think are small and seemingly inconsequential things of life. His entire life reflected commitment.

If we are to show the same commitment toward God that

David did, we will also need to focus on the smallest details, including not only the words we speak but the thoughts we think.

THE POWER OF COMMITMENT

David was committed to God because he knew that God was committed to him. He purposed to commit himself wholeheartedly to obey and honor the Lord. He was determined to praise and glorify Him in good times and bad—in every situation, every day of his life. He would declare his faithfulness to the Lord in one verse, and with the next proclaim God's faithfulness to him.

> *O God, my heart is steadfast;*
> *I will sing and give praise, even with my glory.*
> *Awake, lute and harp!*
> *I will awaken the dawn.*
> *I will praise You, O LORD, among the peoples,*
> *And I will sing praises to You among the nations.*
> *For Your mercy is great above the heavens,*
> *And Your truth reaches to the clouds.*
> PSALM 108:1-4 NKJV

David was humbled by God's faithfulness to him and his heart swelled with gratitude. After all David had walked through with the Lord, he knew God would never let him down. For that reason, he wanted to do all he could to show His Lord that he was deeply grateful and would use his life to bring Him honor. At the end of the day, what more can we do to honor God than to praise Him with our words and deeds?

Of all the attributes that David's life reveals, none is greater than his commitment to God. Throughout the psalms, he clearly states his objective with every "I will" that he declared:

> I will sing of mercy and justice;
> To You, O LORD, I will sing praises.
> I will behave wisely in a perfect way.
> Oh, when will You come to me?
> I will walk within my house with a perfect heart.
> I will set nothing wicked before my eyes;
> I hate the work of those who fall away;
> It shall not cling to me.
> PSALM 101:1-3 NKJV

David was determined to exalt the name of the Lord in his every action whether it be taking down the Philistine giant or honoring his covenant with Jonathan by blessing his son.

David found a variety of ways to celebrate his love for and his commitment to God. He commemorated his Lord on the battlefield with every victory he won. He celebrated with every act of kindness, justice, or mercy he was in a position to bestow. He rejoiced with every friend he blessed. He celebrated God with all the songs he wrote about Him. His life was an example of a man passionately committed to honoring God. So much so, that God referred to him as "a man after his own heart."

> *I will praise You with my whole heart;*
> *Before the gods I will sing praises to You.*
> *I will worship toward Your holy temple,*
> *And praise Your name*
> *For Your lovingkindness and Your truth;*
> *For You have magnified Your word above all Your name.*
> PSALM 138:1-2 NKJV

Imagine the difference it could make in our lives if we were to commit ourselves wholly to God as David did. If we chose to honor Him with every word and deed, what would be the result? We would experience more of God's presence, that is for certain! That would mean more peace, more joy, and more direction. We would also have the satisfaction of knowing that we have honored the One who has sacrificed so much on our behalf.

So the question is, have you experienced the power of God's

commitment to you? If so, are you willing to show that gratefulness of heart by committing yourself wholly to Him so that you might bring glory, honor, and praise to Him?

> *I will extol You, my God, O King;*
> *And I will bless Your name forever and ever.*
> *Every day I will bless You,*
> *And I will praise Your name forever and ever. . . .*
> *I will meditate on the glorious splendor of Your majesty,*
> *And on Your wondrous works.*
> PSALM 145:1-2, 5 NKJV

Heavenly Father,

Your wonderful Word is such a gift, demonstrating your love and commitment to me. Teach me to hear you and to trust you to do what you say, for you always keep your promises.

May I also be a person who keeps my word, who can be trusted. Help me fulfill what I say I will do. Don't let me lie to myself or to you. Help me be honest about my life.

May I always be grateful for your steadfast commitment to me that never changes. May I never take that for granted.

Help me find ways to celebrate my love for you and my commitment to you, today and every day for the rest of my life. May I understand and act on the ways you desire for me to demonstrate my commitment to you— to love mercy, and act justly, and walk humbly with my God.

Thank you for David and his example of what it means to have a heart for you. Thank you for the wonderful life you give me through Christ, now and forever.

Amen.

May the LORD answer you when you are in distress;
may the name of the God of Jacob protect you.
May he send you help from the sanctuary
and grant you support from Zion.
May he remember all your sacrifices
and accept your burnt offerings.

    Selah

May he give you the desire of your heart
and make all your plans succeed.
We will shout for joy when you are victorious
and will lift up our banners in the name of our God.
May the LORD grant all your requests.

Psalm 20:1-5 NIV

· XII ·

David's Prayer for You

From his deathbed, David looked up at Solomon. With all of his heart, he wanted nothing more than for his son to know the joys of God's presence as he himself did— and none of the sorrows of acting in his own foolishness.

The years after Solomon's birth had been harder on David than he thought he could bear. His beloved son Absalom had risen against him, and it tore out David's heart that his own life was spared only at the death of his son. As the prophet Nathan had spoken, the sword had truly not left David's house in all of his remaining years.

David wanted none of that for Solomon, but he would

not be around to protect him. Even now, as he prepared to speak his final words to Solomon, the first threat to Solomon's reign had already emerged. Another of his brothers, Adonijah, had proclaimed himself king. Only by Nathan's intervention and David's quick thinking had Solomon received his father's blessing and been officially crowned instead. What would happen when Solomon faced other such threats alone? David could only hope that his son would cling even more closely to God than he had himself—and that what wisdom David had passed on over the years would rule Solomon's life more than his own lusts and earthly desires.

With these thoughts in mind, David spoke to Solomon:

> "I go the way of all the earth; be strong, therefore, and prove yourself a man. And keep the charge of the LORD your God: to walk in His ways, to keep His statutes, His commandments, His judgments, and His testimonies, as it is written in the Law of Moses, that you may prosper in all that you do and wherever you turn; that the LORD may fulfill His word which He spoke concerning me, saying, 'If your sons take heed to their way, to walk before Me in truth with all their heart and with all their soul,' He said, 'you shall not lack a man on the throne of Israel.'"
>
> 1 KINGS 2:2-4 NKJV

David continued on with specific instructions about

cleansing his house of the men who had done evil in his name and with advice about establishing Solomon's reign with a clean slate before God. Solomon nodded and told his father he would do as instructed.

With that, David closed his eyes, content he had done all he could. He was buried with his fathers in Bethlehem, where one day a descendent would be born who would sit on the throne of Israel forever.

David's final charge to Solomon reflected his deep desire that his son would seek the Lord all of his days. David knew firsthand the benefits and blessings of following God wholeheartedly, and he desired his son to experience those same blessings in his own life.

Likewise, in Psalm 20:1-5 NIV, we see David's desire for those of us who would later follow God. "May the LORD grant all your requests!" (v. 5). When David prayed that God would answer us, he was assuming that we would have a relationship with God where we converse with Him regularly. "May he remember all your sacrifices" (v. 3). David's prayer that God would regard our offerings of praise and thanksgiving suggests first that we should be constantly offering them. "May he give you the desire of your heart" (v. 4). David knew that when we allow God to determine our heart's desire and God then fulfills those plans and purposes, we experience a life worth living.

In essence, David prayed that we would know the God who answers prayer and go to Him often and that nothing in our lives would keep our petitions to the Lord from being heard by Him. David prayed that we would have a relationship with God similar to his—that we would be in constant communication with God, singing songs of praise and worship to our Lord and meditating constantly on His goodness.

We join our prayer with David's now, that you might have a relationship with God like David had and that you would not be satisfied with anything less.

May you lay aside all distractions and pursue the only One worth pursuing—God himself!

Godspeed on your journey.

> *You shall love the Lord your God out of and with your whole heart and out of and with all your soul (your life) and out of and with all your mind (with your faculty of thought and your moral understanding) and out of and with all your strength. This is the first and principal commandment.*
> Mark 12:30 amp